LEADING
TONES

LEADING TONES

REFLECTIONS ON MUSIC, MUSICIANS, AND THE MUSIC INDUSTRY

LEONARD SLATKIN

AMADEUS
PRESS

An Imprint of Hal Leonard LLC

Published in 2017 by Amadeus Press
An Imprint of Hal Leonard LLC
7777 West Bluemound Road
Milwaukee, WI 53213

Trade Book Division Editorial Offices
33 Plymouth St., Montclair, NJ 07042

Printed in the United States of America

Book design by Lynn Bergesen, UB Communications

Library of Congress Cataloging-in-Publication Data

Names: Slatkin, Leonard author.
Title: Leading tones : reflections on music, musicians, and the music
   industry / Leonard Slatkin.
Description: Montclair, NJ : Amadeus Press, 2017. | Includes index.
Identifiers: LCCN 2017019204 | ISBN 9781495091896 (hardcover)
Subjects: LCSH: Slatkin, Leonard. | Conductors—United States—Biography. |
   Music—Anecdotes.
Classification: LCC ML422.S536 A3 2017 | DDC 784.2092 [B]—dc23
LC record available at https://lccn.loc.gov/2017019204

www.amadeuspress.com

For my brother, Fred,
with love, appreciation, and music

Art! Who comprehends her? With whom can one consult con-cerning this great goddess?

—Ludwig van Beethoven

Experience is something you don't get until just after you need it.

—Steven Wright

I don't think of all the misery, but of the beauty that still remains.

—Anne Frank, *The Diary of a Young Girl*

I believe that man will not merely endure: he will prevail. He is immortal, not because he alone among creatures has an inexhaustible voice, but because he has a soul, a spirit capable of compassion and sacrifice and endurance.

—William Faulkner

The key to the mystery of a great artist is that for reasons unknown, he will give away his energies and his life just to make sure that one note follows another . . . and leaves us with the feeling that something is right in the world.

—Leonard Bernstein

For that matter, we're all fools though we don't know it.

—Plautus, *Pseudolus*

CONTENTS

PART ONE

———

LIVING WITH MUSIC

Music expresses that which cannot be said and on which it is impossible to be silent.

—Victor Hugo

OVERTURE

My name is Sherlock Holmes. It is my business to know
what other people do not know.

—Arthur Conan Doyle,
"The Adventure of the Blue Carbuncle"

You never know where life is going to take you. We begin with dreams, and if we are lucky, a few of them come true.

For me, there was never a question of my career path. It was music, music, music. With a family completely immersed in this profession, I was surrounded by the best and the brightest in the field. Occasionally people from other walks of life visited the Slatkin house, but they were few and far between.

When my father suddenly died, I was just nineteen years old, and my life changed. Not that we were close, but his influence on me was profound. My musical hero was gone, and I ceased my instrumental studies. I decided to become a teacher of English literature.

Eventually I came back to the musical fold. But somewhere in the back of my mind there were these little reminders of what might have been. I began to write articles for magazines and newspapers. At first they were amateurish and without a personal voice. Experience and time helped me refine my style.

In 2012 my first book, *Conducting Business*, was published. Very few people knew that I entertained an interest in the printed word, and I did not think any publisher would be interested. Nevertheless, it was received very well, by both the public and journalists, and had stronger sales than usual for a book about classical music. Some of those who encouraged me to write the initial work now wanted more.

Leading Tones is the result.

It had never occurred to me that at least one more book was in the offing. I thought the first tome was it; there was nothing else to say. However, when I went back and began looking at the notes and drafts for the first volume, I found that I had more ideas than could comfortably fit into 300-plus pages.

This time around I have chosen to write about some of my favorite collaborators, the state of the music industry, and odds and ends that I hope you will find interesting.

Although *Conducting Business* contained chapters about some of the people who taught or influenced me, it did not give me enough opportunity to write about the many musicians who were so special to work with. Whether it was Isaac Stern, Nathan Milstein, John Browning, John Williams, or other luminaries in the field, setting down reminiscences of these and other artists seemed a must. As it was not possible to include everyone, I chose just six.

It has been my good fortune to have worked with some of the greatest musicians on the planet. When I began my conducting career in the late 1960s, there were still legends around. Sadly, I never had occasion to collaborate with Horowitz, Rubinstein, Heifetz, or Piatigorsky, although I heard them often and came close to an engagement with each one. Still, I consider myself blessed to have heard them as well as many other musical giants.

In this book I have also tried to define and consider some of the difficulties that have been encountered by so many. Controversy has always surrounded the artistic experience. It was my idea to write in a way that encompassed every side of an issue, whether that meant considering the perspective of female conductors, union leadership, or the orchestral musicians themselves.

During the first part of the twenty-first century, the music business underwent some radical rethinking as well as major paradigm shifts. Some of these concepts were born out of economic necessity, but equally important has been the changing mores of society. In some areas we have become more accepting of the new, but in other ways we are mired in convoluted rules and regulations.

Whether in the area of labor negotiations, audition procedures, discrimination in the workplace, or any number of other topics, there is still a long way to go in remedying the ills that confront us. Yes, we are not as repressive as we were even twenty years ago, but dichotomies and inconsistencies remain in how we conduct business in the arts. Much of this seems at odds with the mostly liberal thinking among artists that pervades the industry. However, it is not always they who have the last word.

Most of what we do is appreciated by a select audience, one with a bit of training that started with their childhood education. It is our job, however, to broaden our reach and make what we do available to as many people as possible. How we teach our children is crucial to growing the arts.

As for actual music making, there are sections devoted to programming and debuts, and even an attempt to choose ten pieces I cannot live without as a conductor. Comparable to my take on the issues confronting the industry as a whole, these selections are highly subjective. They also provide a context in which to view my musical thought process as it has progressed during my life as a conductor.

I both love and hate top 10 lists. They provide a form of entertainment that sometimes can be helpful in sorting out material pertaining to one subject or another. Frequently they are annoying. One must be wary of how they were put together and who was overseeing the project. No such danger in my own compilations. They are highly opinionated, filled with my own preferences.

As with *Conducting Business*, this book is written for the music lover and not just musicians. A little bit of knowledge about music is helpful but not necessary. There are few technical references, and hopefully I have given contextual information where needed.

There are too many people to thank individually. But certainly this book would not be possible if it were not for the diligent work by my assistant, Leslie Karr. My editor was Lawrence B. Johnson, a longtime music journalist and editor of the performing arts web magazine *Chicago on the Aisle*. My wife, Cindy McTee, also aided in uncountable ways during the editing process. Orchestras from all over the world provided material that helped me compile a complete overview of my work. And discussions with musicians, audience members, and patrons of the arts kept me informed as to the varied ways that people think about the cultural scene.

When my musical journeys began, I could not have imagined that they would also encompass publishing words about music. But here we are, two books later, and already the ideas for a third are swirling around my head.

AN AMERICAN
IN LYON

*On this matter I'm inclined to agree with the French, who
gaze upon any personal dietary prohibition as bad manners.*

—Charles Dickens, *A Tale of Two Cities*

In high school I studied French. Lucille Bordman was the teacher and, boy, did she have her hands full. Several of my friends were in the class, and virtually none of us was interested in gender, conjugation, or tenses. About halfway through the third semester, Madame Bordman grew so frustrated with us that she said, "You are like blocks of wood, sitting one next to the other!"

When my conducting activities took me to Europe, my first dates were in the United Kingdom and Germany. France would come a bit later, but those three areas formed the center of my world across the pond. Surprisingly, and without one lesson, I picked up enough German to get by at rehearsals and even manage a few easy conversations. Sometimes I would get into a little verbal trouble and mix up my words. Once, at a department store, while looking for the cashier, I mistakenly asked, "Wo ist die Käse?" rather than *Kasse*. The shop did not have a cheese section.

Early conducting in France was mostly confined to Paris, where I worked with the three major orchestras and also at the Opéra Bastille. The two radio orchestras seemed to provide the best fit. They permitted a bit more flexibility in repertoire than did the Orchestre de Paris at the time. Rehearsals and a few performances took place at the Maison de la Radio, where there were two full-size stages, and one of them also had space for an audience.

Every so often the two ensembles in residence, the Orchestre National de France and the Philharmonique, would be rehearsing at the same time. It was always fun to converse with whoever was conducting the other group, and on one occasion it happened to be Kurt Masur. Our programs could not have been more different. One consisted of music by Schumann, Schubert and Brahms, the other of works by Bernstein and Gershwin.

What made it unusual was that I was the one doing the Austro-German repertoire and Maestro Masur was handling the American works. I popped into one of his rehearsals and could not help but giggle when he told the orchestra that they had to "learn to schving."

Paris was always enjoyable for me. During the early going I was not really into food or wine, but walking around energized me. As in London, you could always duck around the corner and find something you had not seen before. Still, given how many guest dates I had in Berlin, Frankfurt, Bamberg, Munich, Leipzig, and other cities, I was sure that if I got a European post, it would be in Germany.

During one of the Berlin trips, two people came to my dressing room after a concert. One was Anne Poursin, executive director of the Orchestre National de Lyon, and the other was its co-concertmaster, Jennifer Gilbert. I had been to the second city of France a couple of times and had always enjoyed the orchestra but was unprepared for what Madame Poursin said: "We have had some difficulties with the leadership of our orchestra, and we would like to ask if you would consider taking the position."

This literally came out of nowhere. All I could really say was that I was flattered and would speak with my agent and think about what Poursin and Gilbert were proposing. Because I had little knowledge of the city or its arts scene, some investigation was necessary.

The process should have been cut and dried, but there were distractions along the way. As negotiations proceeded, Anne Poursin decided to step down and move to Paris. It was never clear as to why. I felt that I could not go into a job without knowing who my boss would be, so a waiting game ensued that went on for almost two years.

When the dust cleared, the orchestra had parted company with Jun Märkl, who had issues not so much with the orchestra, but with the city. A new executive director, Laurent Langlois, was put in place. He had never run an orchestra before, but when I met with him it seemed like he had a lot of interesting ideas. And in 2011, with things settled, I took the job.

Among the reasons the post appealed to me was the promise of having a second home. I truly disliked all the traveling involved with my guest-conducting appearances. It was one plane and hotel room after another, with no time to really visit the places that were mostly known in my imagination or through pictures, moving and otherwise. Now I could spend sixteen weeks in Detroit and fourteen in Lyon and see a welcome reduction in the number of orchestras I'd be visiting during the season. Also, I could actually have a residence in both cities, and a kitchen without room service.

The Auditorium in Lyon turned forty years old in 2015. It stands in stark contrast to the typical architecture of the city. The exterior looks a bit like a Spielbergian spaceship, but only if the director were having nightmares. Inside things are better. It seats 2,300, and the stage is huge. This made it a bit difficult for the musicians to hear each other well, but after so many years they were used to it. It also boasts one of the most historic pipe organs in the world, played by Saint-Saëns, Franck, and virtually all the other great organists.

For my first concerts as music director, we did not mess around. In one week we performed two different programs, one French and the other featuring Mahler's Second Symphony. Several people from Detroit came for this event. There were posters and signs all over the city announcing my arrival. The festive atmosphere was grand. But very quickly things started to go awry.

Just before the end of his tenure, Jun Märkl and the orchestra were supposed to go to Japan. A few weeks earlier the tsunami had struck, and there were fears that the environment was contaminated to a point that might prove dangerous. None of the scheduled concerts was in the so-called Ring of Fire, but they were close enough to worry the musicians. A face-off ensued, with about half of the orchestra willing to make the trip and the rest wanting to stay home.

Adding fuel to this fire, the city of Lyon—which basically funds everything for the ONL—really wanted the orchestra to serve as its ambassador. The mayor came out against the musicians who refused to go. Langlois went along with the mayor, challenging what was now becoming a majority of the orchestra. (Even though the tour would mark the final concerts of Märkl's directorship, it would also be the start of Langlois's tenure.)

In the end, the tour was canceled, and it was looking doubtful that the ONL would ever be invited to Japan again.

Musically things were going well, but the way the administration was attempting to market its concerts was bizarre. Langlois decided that there needed to be titles for various series. One of them, which featured pieces by French composers, came with the moniker "French Kiss." And yes, it was presented to the public in English. When I asked if the double meaning was clear, no one wanted to comment. Then there was "Invitation to the Dance," though at least two of the programs did not have even one piece related to the theme.

Perhaps worse was the importing of various productions, which cost a great deal and took away from the budget for the orchestra. Money for the next season was reduced, and we had to tighten our belt, even though the ONL had not been a factor in the shortfall. None of this was known to the orchestra or me until we were informed of cutbacks.

We soon pushed Langlois out. This had to be done carefully, since the mayor had appointed him, and it was city hall that would determine our budget in the future. Fortunately, we were starting to jell as a unit, and many of the concerts were sold out. Soloists and guest conductors were eager to come, and not just for the cuisine.

After a search, Jean-Marc Bador came on board as general director. He brought an air of authority but coupled it with a true desire to make peace between the orchestra and the city. We formed a good team, and impressive results followed very quickly. Recordings of the major works of Berlioz and a complete Ravel orchestral cycle commenced. Television was part of the new deal. And reaching the public, through innovative initiatives including an expanded educational role, became part of the mission.

What seemed, when I started, like a provincial ensemble turned into a major force on the French musical scene. What made this orchestra different from others was best summed up by Jean-Marc: "The ONL is a French orchestra with an Anglo-Saxon mentality."

From its founding in 1971 by the French conductor Serge Baudo and continuing through the directorship of his countryman Emmanuel Krivine, who led it from 1987 to 2000, the orchestra enjoyed a strong bond with French music. After the lengthy tenures of these two music directors, David Robertson took over, bringing many innovations to the city. But his strength at the time was really in contemporary music, and the Lyonnaise public did not take to it all that well. Jun Märkl came next and brought a bit more German repertoire to the Auditorium.

Since I had studied with Jean Morel, my own interest in French music went back a long way. I was conversant not only with the usual suspects, but also with some off-the-beaten-track composers from the past. Names like André Caplet, Gabriel Pierné, Jean Roger-Ducasse, and Henri Rabaud would pop up on programs with Debussy and the other kings. Perhaps part of the success of the collaboration was that I came to the ONL with a great deal of experience, rather than learning on the job.

I have often been asked what the difference is between running an orchestra in Europe as opposed to the United States. In Lyon I did not engage in fund-raising directly. As long as I maintained a good relationship with the mayor and other officials, we would do well. The Auditorium is completely under the auspices of city hall, as is a very fine and partly self-sustaining opera company. This creates a little competition, but for the most part the organizations are able to steer clear of each other when it comes to fiscal matters.

During my first two years, while I was getting to know the orchestra, they began to adjust to my direct and compact way of rehearsing. The sound of the orchestra was a bit of a mix. My Russian heritage came into play with a darker and more resonant string sonority. However, the winds, perhaps because they played on instruments made in France, had a slightly lighter and more nasal quality that could only be found in that part of the world.

We usually had four rehearsals plus a dress to get a program prepared, but sometimes, if needed, we could add or subtract. The orchestra played a wildly successful series of programs with film, ranging from Charlie Chaplin to Pixar. The musicians also performed chamber music, often with the guest soloist for the week.

There were irritations. The rehearsal schedule was awkward, if understandable. On Wednesdays students only had a half-day of school, which meant they were home all afternoon and evening. Therefore, in order to keep peace in the players' families, we would rehearse in the morning, ending at noon, and then come back at 8:00 in the evening for another two and a half hours. The problem was that the next morning we were back at it at 9:30.

There were also seemingly interminable meetings. The French do love to talk, and sometimes, with the bar and food in view, more than half an hour would go by as I listened to lengthy speeches and pretended to be fully engaged. When this occurred after a concert, it was a race between my mind and my stomach to see which gave in first.

Cindy and I rented a small apartment that overlooked the Rhône. It was a true neighborhood, with separate shops for bread, cheese, meat, and vegetables. The area was dotted with wonderful little restaurants featuring cuisines from all over the world. The old town is a fine reminder of the history of Lyon, and the Confluence, located where the Rhône and Saône Rivers meet, is a new architectural development area offering a bold glimpse of what will be.

The mayor, Gérard Collomb, has been the kind of political force one desires. He put the city back on the map, not just as a tourist destination, but as one that now attracted major business to the area as well. An "Only Lyon" campaign worked wonders in building bridges outside the Rhône-Alpes region. And of course, Lyon is the birthplace of cinema, making it just a little bit like my childhood city, Hollywood.

We did many major tours, within Europe as well as in Japan, China, and the United States. There were numerous recordings, all of them for the Naxos label. Most important, we were able to increase our overall attendance by more than 30 percent.

So it came as a bit of a shock in December 2015 when I was told that my salary had become an obstacle to my continuing as music director. The mayor's right-hand man went so far as to say in print that "we are looking for someone younger and European." This clearly meant "less expensive." The Auditorium's budget was being cut severely, so I agreed that it was in everyone's best interest for me to step aside. My goals had been accomplished, and as nice as it had been to have a European base, the administrative responsibilities were beginning to weigh heavily on me. The last thing I wanted was for the orchestra to be cut back or hurt in any way.

The same could be said in Detroit, where I had been able to put the orchestra back on track following the six-month strike in 2010–11. Although the Detroit Symphony certainly helped the city move forward, economic difficulties for both the city and the orchestra remained. The ten-year plan to establish a secure endowment was far behind schedule. And, as with Lyon, the burden of a music directorship was taking me away from what I needed to focus on: making music.

Cindy and I have been very fortunate to be part of two institutions that looked forward. Our involvement in those communities was truly a pleasure. I will miss many aspects of my work with the Detroit and Lyon orchestras, but both have made me honorary music director, ensuring that I will conduct several weeks a season with each.

I still regret that I did not learn French as well as everyone had hoped. But I did get better, and this was evident when more and more of the Lyon musicians, staff, and public began speaking to me in their native tongue. Perhaps Madame Bordman is smiling. One of her blocks of wood has finally moved just a bit.

PIECES FOR
A LIFETIME

Music is a continuum, and the modern and avant-garde composers of today will be part of the standard repertoire thirty years from now.

—Sir Neville Marriner

How does one sum up more than fifty years in the public's eyes and ears? At first I thought that just a series of lists, including orchestras I have conducted, my music directorships, and world premieres, would make the most sense. Collaborations that went beyond the norm could be highlighted. Eccentricities and unusual encounters might also be included. But by the time I actually started looking at the sheer number of performances I had led, it was clear that all of this needed more than a mere recitation of statistics.

It all started with pursuing a path that placed American music and its composers in the forefront of my own artistic agenda. The fostering of young talent and the joy of seeing so many of these musicians grow and succeed has been very rewarding. And then there is what seems like a limitless number of recordings.

But let me begin with the world premieres.

There appear to be at least 220, and that is only counting orchestras with which I have had long-term relationships. I chose not to include student or semi-amateur ensembles. Which pieces made it past the first performances? What about their impact on my own career? And which compositions meant the most to me?

St. Louis Symphony Orchestra

The initial work on the list is going to seem very strange. I actually conducted the first live performance of *Jesus Christ Superstar* in April of 1971. This was in St. Louis and occurred because before it was a musical, it was a rock opera, and just a very successful recording, not a Broadway show. When it was decided to turn it into a live work, we were given the opportunity to do it first.

So what makes that important? First of all, we reached an audience that had in many cases never been to a concert in Powell Hall. But conducting *Superstar* was also a timely career move for me. I was still just starting out, and pretty much every orchestra manager in the country showed up to see if the Andrew Lloyd Webber work was feasible for their orchestras. In the process, they watched an unknown young American conductor traverse the piece with relative ease. Several invitations to conduct other orchestras in more standard symphonic fare followed. So the takeaway is to never underestimate how you might reach a wider constituency that can help you in the future.

Sometimes, when we leave our conservatory work behind, we tend to put our teachers on the back burner. I wished to honor them, and so I premiered works by Jacob Druckman, Vincent Persichetti, William Schuman, Peter Mennin, and others who had helped me form my own musical thoughts.

It was Druckman who provoked the most bizarre pre-concert activity I had ever encountered. The place was Chicago, the year was 1989, and the new work was *Brangle*. Outside Orchestra Hall a protest was being held by supporters of the jailed far-right presidential candidate Lyndon LaRouche, who cherished a bizarre antipathy toward modern music of any sort. There were posters of me with a beard and horns painted on. It seems that even unheard new music was indeed the devil's playground. The premiere went on without a hitch, but I can still smell the sulfur and brimstone emanating from the balcony.

Chicago was also the place where I first heard David Del Tredici's *Final Alice*. Although I did not know the composer, I was so knocked out by the piece that immediately after the concert I went backstage, introduced myself, and on the spot commissioned the next Alice work, *In Memory of a Summer Day* (1980). It went on to win the Pulitzer Prize, as did Christopher Rouse's 1992 Trombone Concerto, which I premiered, written for the New York Philharmonic's principal, Joseph Alessi. Virtuosic to a fault, this piece is one of the few to have become standard fare for trombonists. I conducted several other premieres of Chris's works, and I continue to program his music, as do many others.

Bill Bolcom is another composer whose works I have conducted often and all over the world. His eclectic approach to music suits my personality well. In addition to premieres of his flute and clarinet concerti, Fourth and Sixth Symphonies, and other pieces, one of the most memorable concerts I ever led involving his music was at Carnegie Hall in November of 1992 with the St. Louis Symphony. We presented his monumental *Songs of Innocence and of Experience*, a work larger in scope than even Mahler's Eighth Symphony. The performance is still spoken of today. Later I would go on to record that epic, and it garnered four Grammy awards, the most ever captured by a single classical composition.

During my tenure in St. Louis, we had four composers-in-residence. Each worked with the orchestra for three years, and there were at least two original works written during each tenure. First up was Joseph Schwantner, a young man who was starting to make waves on the musical seas. *Magabunda* (1983), a work for soprano and orchestra, was an astonishing vocal showpiece and made huge demands on everyone. It was received rapturously by the public and critics alike. Each of Schwantner's pieces made the rounds of many of the major orchestras, both in the United States and abroad. I was honored to be among the first to single him out.

Next came Donald Erb. His eccentric use of instruments and incredible ear for sonority were hallmarks of his style. My first encounter with his work came via my brother, Fred, who had been principal cellist with the New Jersey Symphony. They had just performed Erb's *The Seventh Trumpet*, and I had never heard Fred more excited by a new work. I immediately engaged Erb in St. Louis, where he wrote several compositions for us. His

Trombone Concerto (1976) and, especially, *Ritual Observances* (1992) are masterpieces. I continued to premiere several works after his St. Louis period ended, including the now-standard Concerto for Brass and Orchestra (1987).

Joan Tower brought her neo-Stravinskian brand of composition to us. Always a delight to work with, Joan is also a real stickler for detail. The orchestra loved her. Her largest work, the Concerto for Orchestra (1991), embodied all her stylistic features. The concerto appears on programs throughout the world. Joan's five (so far) Fanfares for the Uncommon Woman represent the newfound presence of females in the compositional mainstream.

Our final composer from my St. Louis music directorship was Claude Baker. Better known at the time in academic circles, his music served as a buffer between the strict atonalists of the mid-twentieth century and the neo-romantics who surfaced in the 1970s and '80s. *Shadows* (1990) was a piece I often took to other orchestras. Baker's work continued after I departed from St. Louis, and my successor, Hans Vonk, also helped add to the canon.

Other notable premieres during the St. Louis years included works by Peter Schickele, Jerry Goldsmith, Richard Rodney Bennett, John Williams, Steve Reich, Dominick Argento, Terry Riley, and Samuel Adler—as well as six pieces, less notable, from yours truly.

Altogether we presented fifty-two first performances, many of which we took on tour and recorded. We played 164 different pieces by American composers and 144 by living composers, both American and foreign born. It is easy to be proud of this legacy.

There was one quite unusual first performance of a very important piece. Alberto Ginastera began his *Popul Vuh* in 1973 for the Philadelphia Orchestra but did not live to complete the work. After his death in 1983, followed by the passing of the music director Eugene Ormandy a year later, the work was forgotten. I learned of its existence from the pianist Barbara Nissman, and after examining the score I felt that it was in fact complete. In 1989, sixteen years after the commission, *Popul Vuh* finally had its world premiere in St. Louis. It would not be until 2008 that the work would be heard for the first time in the city of its origin, Philadelphia, when I led a performance with the orchestra for which it was intended.

National Symphony Orchestra

It would seem more than obvious that I would use Washington, D.C., as a place to showcase American music, both old and new. We were fortunate to have two patrons who loved underwriting composers. John and June Hechinger enabled me to pursue my vision of making America's capital an even more important part of the country's new music landscape.

Of course, I did commission several of the composers I had championed in St. Louis and knew well. John Corigliano, Schickele, Baker, Bolcom, Richard Danielpour, Tower, and Schwantner all had first performances at the Kennedy Center. But there were many fresh voices as well. Jeffrey Mumford,

Stephen Hartke, Anne LeBaron, Michael Daugherty, Roberto Sierra, Jefferson Friedman, George Tsontakis, Stewart Wallace, and others enlarged my repertoire. But there were a couple that truly stood out, albeit for different reasons.

Later in this book you will learn of a very contentious work, at least according to one critic, by Michael Kamen. Happily, I also commissioned Cindy McTee, who would become my wife many years later, to write her Symphony No. 1, *Ballet for Orchestra* (2002). And Roberto Sierra's *Fandangos* (2000) would go on to be one of the most frequently played new pieces I ever premiered.

After stating in print many years earlier that I really did not like or understand the music of Philip Glass, I wound up commissioning his Symphony No. 7 (2005), for chorus and orchestra. Once I got to know the man and had many discussions with him, my attitude changed dramatically. The symphony was a fine work, and I reacquainted myself with both his earlier and more recent pieces.

Corigliano introduced me to the music of Mason Bates, and I immediately took to it and the composer. My confidence in John's recommendation as well as Mason's talent led me to commission *Liquid Interface* (2007). Along with Michael Tilson Thomas and Riccardo Muti, I would present his music all over the world. It was also during my Washington years that I met Michel Camilo. We have worked together many times, and his First Piano Concerto (1998) was premiered by the NSO and me.

Yet there was a downside to my musical adventures with the National Symphony. Hearing fifty-nine first performances, as well as 179 different American works, 105 of them by living

composers, may have been a bit too much for the Washingtonians. This all took place over twelve seasons, or two Senate
terms. The one thing that I know everyone loved was an
American Festival in which, over the course of six programs
in two weeks, we presented eighteen versions of "The Star
Spangled Banner." Many of these transcriptions were made by
conductors who did not originally come from America.

Detroit Symphony Orchestra

Following my term limit in Washington, the next ten years
were spent as music director in Detroit, a city and orchestra
then undergoing extraordinarily difficult economic times. This
represented America's heartland, home of the automobile as
well as Orchestra Hall, one of the country's great acoustical
marvels. There were high hopes all around, but the first three
years proved to be problematic.

During my first season, I was still wrapping up things in
Washington and could only conduct five subscription concerts.
The next year, 2009, I had a heart attack and was out of commission for three months. And the third season—well, there
was no third season. The orchestra went on strike, one of several
work stoppages by major orchestras that year.

Now my mission of advancing American music and building
on a fine artistic institution had changed. Instead of forging
ahead with an agenda driven entirely by artistic considerations,
my associates at the DSO and I had to pick up the pieces and get
the orchestra back on a positive track. Already in place was an

annual gift that allowed a work by a female composer to be premiered each season. Creative minds on our staff figured out ways to commission new works without spending outrageous sums. And my own relationships with composers helped secure some very important and interesting pieces during the final seven seasons.

There were twenty-nine world premieres from an extremely diverse group of composers. These included nine compositions by women and three written by African Americans. We had pieces from the Arab world and Asia. In addition, there were numerous works from the past, most of them never before heard in Detroit, that sprang from American pens.

Perhaps the most controversial work we performed was a multimedia project conceived by MIT's Tod Machover. Symphony in D (2015) was meant to be a celebration of the city. Tod spent many weeks in Detroit, recording the sounds that he heard from factories, the street, and just about anywhere he encountered something interesting. These were incorporated into other prerecorded materials that played as the piece progressed.

In addition, Tod placed several live components within the work itself. These included poets, a group of seniors, a Chaldean choir, and some budding DJs. With all this material, as well-meaning as the project was, the orchestra seemed to be secondary to the proceedings. Still, it was heartening to see the warm response accorded to the various performers on the stage when the work concluded.

Other notable premieres included David Del Tredici's only opera, *Dum Dee Tweedle* (1991), a work that had lain dormant for more than twenty years. It had been given a piano read-through, but the composer never got around to orchestrating it. There was Alla Borzova's *Songs for Lada* (2009), written to Belarusian texts and featuring indigenous instruments, two female soloists, and children's choir. The Spanish composer Ferran Cruixent gave us two pieces that incorporated very unusual orchestral techniques, none more arresting than having each musician download a prerecorded ringtone and play it back during the performance.

But probably the most interesting premiere was not so much about the piece as about where it was premiered. When the Arab American composer Mohammed Fairouz gave us a new cello concerto in 2016, I decided to have it played not at Orchestra Hall but at the largest synagogue in the area. The melding of styles and the venue seemed perfectly natural, and I was proud of this multicultural outreach.

BBC Symphony Orchestra

With my two directorships in Europe, I continued my quest to present American music to the widest possible audiences. But this path had to be different. Essentially, these audiences only knew the names Bernstein, Gershwin, Barber, Ives, and Copland. The so-called minimalist school had caught the fancy of some, so there were performances of Glass, John Adams, and Steve Reich, but most of our other composers were new territory.

The BBC Symphony prides itself on the number of new works it presents each year. It is impossible to estimate how many, but certainly more than any other orchestra in the world. Numerous composers have been promoted by this orchestra's extraordinary commitment.

We had worked together a few times prior to my becoming chief conductor, and already there were premieres to be given. Through four years as chief conductor, my numbers might pale in comparison to some others, but still it was a huge adventure. With an output of new music this large, it would be interesting for someone to find out how many of these commissions actually entered the repertoire.

My first premiere with the Beeb was not a particularly happy occasion. The piece was called *The Red Act Arias* (1997), by the American composer Roger Reynolds. It was scored for narrator, chorus, and orchestra, and the whole thing was manipulated by electronic gadgetry located in the middle of the Albert Hall. What I saw on the page bore very little semblance to what was actually being heard, and at one point, so I was told, I lost my temper. This does not occur very often, so something must have really gotten me upset and frustrated. To this day, I have little recollection of either my fit of pique or the piece.

Most of the remaining twelve first performances took place at the Proms. There is always a new work for the Last Night, and isolated pieces pop up, too. Music by Mark-Anthony Turnage, Dominic Muldowney, Alexander Goehr, Joseph Phibbs, and Judith Weir, among others, were presented. There was a fitting emphasis on British music, both old and new. To that end, perhaps the most unusual presentation came during a performance at Maida Vale, the studio where the orchestra rehearses and occasionally does concerts. It was not a premiere but a second performance of the Concerto for Piano (1938) by one Alan Bush.

He was an important British composer but also a highly controversial political figure. He was against England's entering World War II, and this piece, with baritone soloist and chorus, entertains a kind of Lenin-in-London scenario. At the premiere the performers broke out into the national anthem directly following the last note, as if to head off any patriotic rioting. It is hard to remember much about this work other than that the piano part was ferociously difficult.

Still, I was pleased with how well we did with American music. Twenty-five works were played, and fifteen of those composers were living at the time. Considering that my predecessors included Pierre Boulez, perhaps my taste was too conservative for the Brits.

Orchestre National de Lyon

In Lyon the emphasis was clearly French. With a wide range of French composers taught to me by Jean Morel, and with my two immediate predecessors not really into this music, I had an upper hand. We reveled in Ravel, bounced along with Berlioz, and danced with Debussy. But I still brought a strong American presence and produced a three-week festival devoted to the music of the United States.

We only gave four world premieres during my six-year tenure, and two of those were reconstituted works by Ravel.

Thirty-three pieces by American composers (twenty-four of them still alive) made it a rewarding achievement. We even performed *4'33"* by John Cage, a piece consisting of nothing but the ambient sounds of the listening space.

Minnesota Orchestra

The two other orchestras with which I had a strong connection to new music were in New York and Minnesota. I created and for ten years led the Minnesota Orchestra's Sommerfest, but prior to that we had an adventurous set of "Rug" concerts, similar to what Boulez was doing in New York. The seats were covered with platforms, and the audience brought rugs and pillows—not to mention other substances—while we played some very unusual pieces. I was also the orchestra's principal guest conductor, so our connection went on for many years.

During my time in Minnesota we gave eleven premieres, the most notable among them Steven Stucky's *Dreamwaltzes* (1986). But we also played eighty-seven works by American composers and sixty-one by living composers. Probably the most memorable was the *Poème symphonique* by György Ligeti. This work is scored for one hundred metronomes, fortunately not the electronic kind. Tables were set up, and ten of us unleashed the timekeeping devices, turning the wind-up knob just twice. At first it was sort of mesmerizing, but the real fun began as the piece wound down. Two of the metronomes were left standing, ticking slowly away until one of them finally gave up the ghost, after which the other had just one more click to victory.

New York Philharmonic

The New York Philharmonic, along with the Boston Symphony, probably has the best track record when it comes to new music for an orchestra in the United States. After all, several of its music directors were also distinguished composers. Some of my Philharmonic premieres have already been mentioned and were by composers I had worked with several times. The list also includes Robert Beaser, Bernard Rands, Toru Takemitsu, John Zorn, and Tan Dun.

Over a forty-year period I presented 139 works by American composers, sixty-two of them alive at the time, with the New York Philharmonic. A sad oddity was that in 1990 I conducted works of Leonard Bernstein both while he was living and then a few days after he died. I also led memorial pieces with this orchestra honoring William Schuman, Aaron Copland, and Morton Gould.

Pittsburgh Symphony Orchestra

The Pittsburgh Symphony, for which I served as principal guest conductor, had a composer-in-residence each year. Although the music director usually did the majority of the premieres, I had the pleasure of presenting four of them. The most notable was the Violin Concerto by Mason Bates (2012). The piece has now been played by orchestras all over the world.

With statistics compiled from thirty-six different orchestras, the basic numbers through the 2017–18 season are as follows:

World premieres: 220
Works by American composers: 1,204
Works by living composers: 754

The thirty-five professional orchestras embraced in this list include all five in London; the Halle; the Berlin Philharmonic and the Deutsches Symphonie; the Amsterdam Concertgebouw, Netherlands Philharmonic, and Rotterdam Philharmonic; orchestras in Hamburg, Frankfurt, Cologne, and Milan; and the three orchestras in Paris. The only Asian orchestra included in this list is the NHK in Tokyo.

In the United States, besides the orchestras I have served as music director, the list includes New York, Boston, Philadelphia, Cleveland, Chicago, Pittsburgh, Cincinnati, Seattle, Los Angeles, San Francisco, Atlanta, Dallas, Houston, Nashville, Chicago's Grant Park Music Festival, and Minnesota.

With each of those orchestras, there was also a very healthy representation of the symphonic canon. Among the standard works I performed most often, there were no big surprises:

Beethoven: Seventh Symphony
Brahms: Fourth Symphony
Tchaikovsky: Fifth Symphony
Schumann: Third Symphony
Mendelssohn: Fifth Symphony
Berlioz: *Symphonie fantastique*
Ravel: *Daphnis et Chloé* Suite No. 2
Mahler: Symphony No. 1

  Shostakovich: Symphony No. 5
  Prokofiev: Symphony No. 5

And as noted earlier, the Barber *Adagio for Strings* was easily the most performed short piece, if one does not include the innumerable presentations of "The Stars and Stripes Forever (and Then Some!)"—usually played as an encore.

Another perspective on my career path is provided by audio recordings in many formats, including LPs, eight-track cartridges, cassette tapes, CDs, DVDs, and, more recently, downloads as well as streaming.

I made recordings for twenty different record companies, and those do not include orchestras that started their own independent labels. The first discs came out in 1975, coincidental with the season when I made my big splash with international orchestras. It was the first complete set of all the orchestral music of Gershwin, with the pianist Jeffrey Siegel. Vox Records really wanted this project and felt that the then music director in St. Louis, Walter Susskind, was not the right conductor. Susskind most generously allowed me to tackle it, and the set garnered spectacular reviews and sales. It remains in the catalog to this day.

With St. Louis, I recorded complete sets of the music of Rachmaninoff as well as all the film scores by Prokofiev. Among the first of the budget labels, Vox was able to show strong profits from these efforts, and it was a pleasure to work with them. After a couple of years other companies starting showing interest in us, and we made many discs for Telarc, EMI, Nonesuch, BMG, and New World. For all of these we also recorded a significant amount of American music, both old and new.

The late 1970s and early '80s were the final great years for the classical recording industry. In St. Louis alone, we were producing an average of four discs each season. There were complete cycles of Tchaikovsky symphonies and ballets, a great deal of Copland and Barber, and even more Gershwin. Virtually all the music with orchestra by Rachmaninoff, including the works with chorus and piano, was recorded. But there was also a balance of repertoire divided up among these labels. Brahms, Mahler, Schubert, and Shostakovich were among the composers we committed to disc. When St. Louis won its first Grammy, in 1984, for a recording of Prokofiev's Fifth Symphony, it sent a shock wave throughout the industry. No one seemed surprised about the quality of the recording, but up to that point these awards usually went to more celebrated ensembles.

We continued to promote other American composers as well, with all four of our composers-in-residence—Schwantner, Erb, Tower, and Baker—represented by at least a disc apiece. Music of Bolcom, Druckman, and Corigliano sat alongside that of Piston, Schuman, and Ives. It was a very special time.

This coincided with my early regular appearances with orchestras in London. Over a period of about twelve years, I was able to record complete cycles of the symphonies of Vaughan Williams, most of the major works of Elgar and Walton, and the last symphonies of Haydn—his "London" series. Newly emerging labels became interested, and some of my output could be found on Varèse Sarabande and Virgin Classics as well as BMG (formerly RCA).

There were even some projects in Germany and France, including five operas as well as some Richard Strauss and Paul Dukas. I had moved from St. Louis to Washington, D.C., and it looked as if the number of recordings would continue as they had. But fiscal reality started to come into play. The buying market was just not there anymore, and with so much product now available, many of us who had lucrative contracts were dropped from various rosters.

But the smaller labels continued on, and I could freelance, making fewer discs than before, but still enough to see at least one release every year. In 1987 the music world was turned upside down by an enterprising German who founded a Hong Kong–based label called Naxos. Klaus Heymann started recording virtually everything possible, using lesser-known artists and orchestras, and selling the discs at bargain-basement prices. This drove the larger companies crazy, because Heymann realized that at this time, the public was driven not so much by the artists as by the repertoire. Why spend up to $60 for a set of the Beethoven symphonies on Deutsche Grammophon when Naxos could sell it for $20 or less?

A lot of people did not trust or like Heymann's philosophy, but I found it intriguing. Thus began a very long and fruitful relationship with the company, resulting in my ability to record much-neglected music as well as some core repertoire. What other company would have taken a chance on putting out five volumes devoted to the music of Leroy Anderson? Sure, Naxos did not pay much at all, and they retained the rights to all the recorded material for what seemed like an eternity, but to me it was just a matter of getting music out to the public and not worrying so much about a profit margin.

In order to counter the Naxos surge, many orchestras began to create their own labels, mostly issuing recordings taken from concerts with a bit of patching done to eliminate audience noise and the occasional misstep from orchestra or conductor. When the strike ended in Detroit, we began doing the same, issuing the complete symphonies of Tchaikovsky, Brahms, and Beethoven. The DSO's relationship with Naxos also spawned my second Rachmaninoff cycle, a series of the full-length Copland ballets, and an ongoing set of the concertos by John Williams (all featuring musicians of the DSO as soloists), in addition to music by McTee and Borzova. In Lyon we also worked with Heymann to record virtually all the Ravel works utilizing orchestra—ten discs in all—as well as most of the major works of Berlioz.

It is pretty much impossible to come up with statistics for all this recording activity amid the confusion of compilations, what counts as a single work or a set of short pieces, and discs that were only issued in one specific country. But I can at least give you a few facts and stories that I hope you find interesting and perhaps amusing.

I have recorded Mussorgsky's *Pictures at an Exhibition* six times, two of them in the traditional Ravel version and the others as compilations of orchestrations by others. There is even one that includes my own adaptations based on the original Mussorgsky and Ravel's orchestration.

There are three separate recordings of the Barber *Adagio for Strings*. The timings vary from 7:28 to 7:45 to 9:08. But the most satisfying and moving one is only available on YouTube, from the Last Night of the Proms. The performance took place in 2001, just four days after 9/11, and clocks in at 10:31. My father's wonderful recording is timed at 7:45.

The St. Louis Symphony recording of the complete *Sleeping Beauty* of Tchaikovsky took three years to finish. Whenever we had time left over after finishing a larger work, we would just continue with bits of *Sleeping Beauty*, injecting the various components into place until the ballet was complete.

I recorded four sound tracks with pickup orchestras. The first was for *The Exorcist,* and the second was for a film called *Red Sky at Morning*. This was followed by the classical music used in a remake of *Unfaithfully Yours*, and last was the John Corigliano score for *Edge of Darkness*. After a full week of work, the producer rejected the music, and it was not used in the released version of the film. But there is a recording of the sound track floating around somewhere.

I have made, at best guess, about 250 separate recordings. There have been seven Grammys and sixty-four nominations. My parents won Grammys in 1958, the very first year the award was presented.

The last point is more of an answer to a question that pops up now and again: "Do you prefer studio recording or live-performance recording taken from concerts?"

My answer is that both are demanding. In a way the studio conditions are a bit easier. When you have, for example, three performances on separate days, you start thinking about the tempi, phrasings, and the like that you did during the prior performance. So it is a bit harder to be spontaneous. In the studio you can start and stop as needed. However, I always make sure that we have one or two complete takes of a whole work to use as a reference point.

A recording is really nothing more than a snapshot of how the performers played on a given day. It has been instructive, in rerecording some of the repertoire, to see how much my own view of a work may have changed.

And usually, once one of my recordings has been issued, I never listen to it again unless it pops up on a radio station. This has unfortunate consequences if I turn the station on in the middle of the piece: Usually I don't like the performance—only to learn that it's mine!

THE TEN

Lists are anti-democratic, discriminatory, elitist, and sometimes the print is too small.

—David Ives

Possibly the most-despised question musicians are asked is, "What is your favorite piece of music?" We usually smile bravely and say something such as, "The one I am performing at the time," or, "It is not possible to have a favorite."

But inside, each and every one of us knows which works move us in very special ways. Some refer to these as "desert island" pieces. Listeners have them, and so do performers. Yes, we try to give our all in each composition we present, but there are always a few pieces that we push ahead a percentage point or two.

I decided to tackle the query but in a slightly different way. Instead of simply trying to list my favorite works to hear, I've opted to explore the music I most enjoy conducting. I certainly love listening to the pieces selected, but there is something special about actually leading them.

Sure enough, I came up with my own top ten, those compositions that have given me exceptional pleasure over a long career. In some cases the choices were obvious, but in a few others the selections might seem unusual. Keep in mind that much of this has to do with the physical, mental, and emotional challenges inherent in the pieces. The list is not about what I consider to be the greatest compositions ever written.

There is no Baroque music and nothing by any living composer. How was it possible to leave out the Bach B Minor Mass? Simply because I have only conducted it one time and felt that I was completely inadequate to the work's enormous import. And it would not be fair to include any of my contemporaries for fear of alienating some of my best friends.

No Mahler? This no doubt seems surprising in this day and age; yet even as I appreciate a good Mahler performance, most of the time I come away with a greater sense of accomplishment than insight. There was a time when I hated this composer, but the years have seen me embrace his music.

Others I left off include Stravinsky, Hindemith, Schumann, Ives, Debussy, and Vaughan Williams, all composers I adore. When you are limiting yourself to ten, the selection process guarantees that there will be many regrettable omissions. And I did not want to create a runner-up category.

Here are the pieces I have chosen, with commentary on why they mean so much to me as a conductor:

Beethoven: Symphony No. 3, "Eroica"

The inclusion of this masterpiece is automatic. I cannot imagine any conductor leaving it out. The voyage of discovery, no matter how many performances one gives, is unique.

Where does one start? During the study process, an understanding of the work's history as well as the social, cultural, and political conditions of the time is crucial. When you arrive for rehearsals, there is no time to explain everything to the orchestra, but you must show how immersed you are in the drama that is the "Eroica."

There are few opening measures that so decisively set the tone for an almost hourlong piece. The two hammer-blow chords that Bernstein described as shattering the conventions of the symphony can be interpreted in many ways. Over the years I have gone from feeling the grandeur of this opening passage to experiencing its stark energy—literally an explosion of fury being unleashed. For me, it has to do with the fact that the same two chords will also close the movement, although the orchestration at that point is slightly different.

Setting the tempo is critical. Works that are cast as formal symphonies require strict attention to any material that recurs during the course of the first movement. The sonata-form structure of the first movement cannot be tampered with. The first and second themes, for example, need to be played at the same speed when they recur. So a constant awareness of tempo relationships is crucial.

When I was younger, my own tempi for this movement tended to be rather lingering. These days I feel the forward thrust and momentum almost constantly. This is not a concession to historically informed performance practice but rather a feeling that the structure can collapse if the speed sags. It is also because of this brisk tempo that I now take the exposition repeat, something I never did in almost forty years of conducting the work.

The crunching dissonances, the unexpected horn entry just before the exposition repeat, and the abrupt key changes all continue to amaze me. How is it even possible to imagine what audiences made of this music at its premiere? It still shocks today.

One is left exhausted after the opening movement, but then comes the even-more-daunting funeral march. Beethoven leaves no doubt that this is the emotional heart of the work. Some people believe that it was in his Second Symphony that the composer started to place more importance on the slow movement, but it is truly with the "Eroica" that this innovation takes hold.

Leaving aside the various discussions about the reliability of Beethoven's own metronome markings or his inability to hear it when he put the markings in the score, one must go by what the music appears to mean. It is designated "Marcia funebre." That is really what must be conveyed. So for me, this means a slow, deliberate pace.

What always gets to me in the second movement is the extraordinary double fugue about halfway through. This achingly beautiful passage is so full of energy and emotion that it is impossible not to get caught up in the pathos created. There are moments of repose followed by volcanic dynamic outbursts. It is as if there is no relief. Even during those few moments when the atmosphere is calm, we know that there will be tumult to follow.

The third movement seems to bounce along at a jaunty clip, with irregular phrasings throwing off the balance. When we arrive at the trio, appropriately scored for three horns, we are placed in a German forest, with the hunters triumphantly celebrating an uncertain victory. Even the return of the scherzo brings a new idea, with misplaced rhythmic bars in two instead of three beats.

The coda leads almost directly into the finale, with a dizzying whirl of sound from the strings. After a pause, and when the first-time listener believes that there is more angst ahead, Beethoven gives us the simplest of tunes. Pizzicati alternate with short notes in the woodwinds, signaling the start of an elaborate set of variations.

As these develop, two more fugues are presented; the ultimate complexity of the last movement exceeds that of Mozart's "Jupiter" Symphony. Never before had a last movement had the depth or breadth found here. A lengthy andante interrupts the seeming riot, and just as the music appears to fade away, a brilliant coda erupts, sending the performers and listeners hurtling back to the energy of the first movement. Exhaustion is evident on the face of every musician and, if the performance has been successful, that of many audience members as well.

This is a work of constant amazement, with every bar as monumental as the symphony's subject matter. I suppose it is possible to come off the concert platform with a feeling of elation, but for me, the best I can do is say to myself that perhaps I got a little closer to the truth.

Berlioz: *Roméo et Juliette*

Here is a piece that is not performed often, and yet it encapsulates all the elements that make this composer special. It has the madness of the *Symphonie fantastique*, the solo vocal beauty of *Les nuits d'été* and the choral power of the Requiem. The forces needed to mount the work are not gargantuan. So why the neglect?

Perhaps part of the problem is identifying exactly what kind of piece this is. The composer and others labeled it a "Dramatic Symphony," but what that actually means is unclear. Certainly the work started life as a possible opera, but Berlioz had even grander ambitions.

"This is going to be something truly unique," he wrote. "A libretto for a symphony! An orchestra to represent an opera!"

And so it was that in 1839, Berlioz outdid Beethoven, whose Ninth Symphony had been premiered just fifteen years earlier. There is no question that the German masterpiece was the template for much of *Roméo*. But the scale and scope of the new work were unlike anything that had come before.

It is not a recreation of the play. The text comes from Émile Deschamps and can be divided into three distinct parts. A synopsis of the story is told in the prologue, which is scored for orchestra, small choir, and two soloists. There are moments when the text reflects on actions of the play as well as actual quotes from Shakespeare.

The majority of the work is given over to several large orchestral scenes, including three movements that correspond to the traditional introduction-and-allegro, slow movement, and scherzo of symphonic form. An elaborate choral finale caps it all off and introduces a baritone soloist taking the role of Friar Lawrence.

My father was obsessed with Toscanini. It was the Italian maestro's version of *Roméo et Juliette* that our family constantly listened to at home, with Dad marveling at the virtuosity of the playing during the Queen Mab Scherzo.

"That is how an orchestra should always sound," he used to proclaim.

During my student years at Juilliard, Jean Morel led performances of the Romeo Alone episode and the Festival at the Capulets' movement. It made a profound impression, as the majority of Berlioz's music was unknown to me. Here was a piece full of emotion, color, and vibrancy. Morel would spend hours talking about the full symphony. And to see on the page what I had listened to quite a few years before was transformational. It is one thing to hear a work and another to actually look at the notes. This is similar to seeing a Shakespeare play and then reading it, finding all those marvelous details that might have passed by unnoticed.

When I first conducted the work in St. Louis, it seemed overwhelming. Had I bitten off more than I could chew? But the effort was worth it, and I found myself physically in tune with the piece. The difficulties seemed less complex than I had imagined, and my own instincts kicked in when I tried to make the work seem like a true symphony. The disparate elements were connected. The somewhat sprawling finale felt totally natural.

How could one not be seduced by the extraordinary Love Scene? The magic of Mab was like flickering sparks igniting. Juliette's funeral cortege felt like a model of simplicity and complexity at the same time. Friar Lawrence's sermon of reconciliation was the only logical conclusion to the piece.

Despite, or because of, the unusual formal structure, *Roméo* has always been one of those pieces I most look forward to conducting. There is always the pleasure of discovering something unseen. The finale mellows the sense of the tragedy, but perhaps I find more connection with the title characters in the way they are portrayed by Berlioz. In the end, it is all exhausting and exhilarating.

Brahms: Serenade No. 1

Of course I love the symphonies, concerti, and overtures, but this work has become quite special to me. Perhaps it is because even in this early work we hear the composer's voice, albeit in a much simpler vein than we expect with the mature ones. Surprisingly, there are not that many works, excluding the ones with chorus, in which Brahms actually utilizes an orchestra: four symphonies, four concerti, two overtures, three Hungarian dances, the Haydn Variations, and two serenades. That's it. Just sixteen pieces.

But what amazing works they are.

The First Serenade began life as a nonet for winds and strings. It was then converted to Brahms's first true orchestral piece, the First Piano Concerto, which was performed a few days before the premiere of the serenade. The work was not a huge success, but the public already had a great deal of respect for the composer, so they were politely appreciative. Struggling to come to grips with the specter of Beethoven, Brahms would wait almost twenty-five years before finally writing a symphony. The two serenades, as well as the First Piano Concerto, were warm-ups for the challenge ahead.

The scoring is modest, with winds in pairs, four horns, two trumpets, timpani, and strings—almost Beethovenian in its forces. What makes the structure of the serenade unusual is that it is cast in six movements, not unlike what Mozart did in his serenades. There is no attempt to relate the musical material thematically between each movement, a practice Brahms would not begin until arriving at the Third Symphony.

The first movement starts in the simplest of ways: just the drone of low strings against a horn solo. The structure is cast in an almost traditional sonata-allegro form, although the coda is unusual in its indefinite ending. The first of three scherzi takes us into harmonically adventurous territory with a dark, brooding theme, quite advanced chromatically. The trio section is more boisterous, fading at the end and leading quite naturally back to the first section.

Then we come to the true glory of the piece, the heartbreaking Adagio in B-flat. Since the whole work is in D major, this shocking key brings us to a new world of astonishing beauty. Beginning the movement with the low strings and varying the colors throughout, Brahms is at his melodic best. The amply effective scoring belies the small forces. This movement, the longest of the whole piece, is a work of genius.

No single place is more poignant than a moment that occurs just after the recapitulation. To make the transition between the two main themes, Brahms gives us an incredible shift in keys, punctuated by a remarkable and unique piece of orchestration. The device used is called a "circle of fifths," where the harmonic element moves from one key to the next in degrees of five notes over the bass line. Usually this is done just by having some of the instruments play the low notes as they would come in the sequence. But Brahms does it in a most unusual and moving manner. The tune is played by the upper woodwinds and violas, with a countermelody in the first bassoon and celli, accompanying figures in the violins, and the circle of fifths in the basses and second bassoon. Notice that there is no mention of brass. They do not play at all during these eight measures, and yet it seems as if the whole orchestra is singing its collective heart out. It is impossible to describe the feeling that comes over me when I get to this point in the piece.

The next scherzo begins with just two clarinets and bassoon. The trio is for strings alone. The fifth movement brings most of the forces back into play and starts as if going on a hunting expedition. Once again horns play a prominent role, both at the start of the piece and again in the trio.

The finale is a romp that could almost be out of Schubert. It also gives us a little hint of what is to come in Brahms's Second Symphony. Heroic on one hand and wistful on the other, it is the logical conclusion to a magical piece. I hope that someday the public takes to the two serenades as they do the symphonies and concerti.

Schubert: Symphony No. 9 in C Major

This monumental opus remains pivotal. The nickname "Great" applies for several reasons. It differentiates this piece from Schubert's more modestly framed Sixth Symphony, also in C major. The sheer scope of the work is unlike any that had been written before. It also presages the grand symphonic edifices to come by Bruckner, Mahler, and many others.

To me, this symphony represents the perfect bridge between the classical formality of Mozart and Haydn and the soon-to-be-flourishing romanticism of Brahms and Schumann. The instrumentation is not huge: no percussion, just woodwinds in pairs along with two horns, two trumpets, three trombones, timpani, and strings. But the sound that emerges exceeds the size of the ensemble. Beethoven is clearly the model; the symphony was written just before the great German composer died.

As with most music written in the late stages of the Classical era, it is paramount to have the tempo of each movement firmly in your head and body before giving any indication to the orchestra. In these days of revisionist thinking regarding some repertoire, tempi have become a bit on the quick side. I hark back to performances that I listened to when I was young. Those were generally more spacious than renditions we hear today, and my performances are more of a throwback to that time. Since we do not have metronome markings from Schubert, it really is up to the individual conductor to decide how fast or slow something will proceed.

The unusual opening, utilizing just the two horns, sets a lyric stage for what will become a work of high drama. At around fifty-five minutes, this was the longest purely symphonic work at the time of its writing. The satisfaction of a good performance comes from the feeling of inevitability when you arrive at the final bar. What started off as something simple becomes a journey of immense complexity.

It is crucial to keep all the tempo relationships in mind while conducting this piece. Certainly many of us will hold back some sections and move others forward, but we all have to keep the formal structure in mind throughout. When Schubert brings back the introductory horn tune, it must feel as if we had heard it several times during the first movement, although in actuality this melody only appears in the opening section.

George Szell used to say that the second movement was the most difficult of all pieces to begin conducting. I can see his point. Like Beethoven's "Eroica," the center of the whole work is concentrated here. There is an almost marchlike feeling to the start of this movement and many alterations of musical material. The climax is not one that is actually played, but rather an extraordinary silence. There must be a total suspension of time, with the audience almost on the edge of their seats wondering what comes next.

The scherzo certainly anticipates Bruckner in that it does not provide relief from what has come before. Although almost peasantlike, the music displays Mendelssohnian grace, especially in the trio. We are also aware of Schubert's unique use of the trombones.

And that finale? Violinists love the symphony until they get to this movement. The sheer physical demand on the players' bow arms, with very little respite, is a challenge to virtually everyone.

Ravel: *L'enfant et les sortilèges*

As with Berlioz's *Roméo et Juliette*, this piece seems to summarize everything the composer was about. With its astonishing orchestral palette, it has color to burn. The vocal writing is superb throughout, and the conclusion is one of the most heartrending in the entire repertoire.

As a child I had an early recording of this opera and was enchanted by the story as well as the music. It remained on my radar throughout my career, but I did not have the opportunity to perform it until my directorship of the National Symphony Orchestra. After that, the only other performance I led was in Lyon. Both of these were concert versions, although the Washington performance was semistaged.

For a few years I taught an orchestration class at Washington University in St. Louis. Instead of using a textbook, I informed the students that we would be learning from three scores: Beethoven's Third Symphony, Tchaikovsky's complete *Nutcracker*, and Ravel's *L'enfant et les sortilèges*. As a manual for learning how to write for orchestra, these pieces contain pretty much everything you need to know through the first part of the twentieth century.

In forty-five minutes Ravel runs the gamut of emotion, color, and drama. Opening with two oboes playing in fifths in the upper register, the opera reveals a world that is both exotic and unique. Throughout the piece, there are surprises galore. A *luthéal* inserted into the piano replicates harpsichord, cimbalom, and otherworldly effects.

There are jazz elements, as evidenced by a foxtrot for teapot and saucer. Two cats have an unlikely duet, with lots of glissandi for both animals and orchestra. A clock, which has been damaged by the protagonist, tries unsuccessfully to keep time. The shepherds on the wallpaper come to life and deliver a French Renaissance song. The animals in the forest sing various syllables to represent frogs, birds, and other creatures. There is even a slide whistle. The invention never ends.

But perhaps the most moving passage, and one that I cite as my favorite moment in any opera, is the closing chorus. The animals have forgiven the child for his aggressive behavior, mainly because they see the human quality of compassion in the boy. This choral setting is extraordinarily beautiful. The two oboes return with their simple utterance of the fifths that opened the opera. And then the child ends the work with one word: "*Maman*." If this does not melt your heart, then I would have to wonder what would.

Barber: Symphony No. 1

When American symphonists are spoken of, names such as Schuman, Copland, Roger Sessions, Walter Piston, Roy Harris, and even Ives come up. Very rarely is Samuel Barber mentioned, perhaps because he only wrote two pieces in the genre—and he rejected the second one. But this first work is among the very finest symphonies in the repertoire.

At the age of twenty-six Barber was already a highly respected composer whose advocates included Arturo Toscanini, Artur Rodzínski, and Bruno Walter. The symphony was written in France and premiered in Rome in December 1936—an appropriate venue, because of all the American composers of his generation, Barber was easily the most European in his musical thought. Romanticism flowed from his pen. This certainly accounted for his rejection by a number of musicians and journalists as the years progressed and what would become known as modernism, as exemplified by Anton Webern, became the new music championed by many.

Sadly, this symphony has not really entered the standard repertoire, which also can be said of most American works using traditional symphonic structure. I try to perform the piece often, not infrequently as the first performance by a given orchestra.

At about twenty minutes in length, Barber's symphony certainly does not present itself as an overblown statement. Essentially, it is a one-movement work divided into four sections roughly corresponding to the movements of a traditional symphony. The whole piece consists of just three thematic elements, each of which is used throughout the work. The transformation of these themes is masterly. Barber audaciously casts his finale as a passacaglia in E minor, the same form and key Brahms used in his Fourth Symphony.

The slow movement contains one of the most eloquent oboe solos in the repertoire, based on the second theme of the first

movement. There is an almost Sibelius-like quality to this section: rich brass playing in C major with the melody now given
in unison to the strings. The scherzo is a fast version of the
opening melody, completely disguised until one analyzes the
pattern. And the first section sets all of this up.

Among the reasons I have chosen this as one of my favorite
pieces to conduct is that orchestras always say to me, "We don't
know why we haven't played this before." And audiences have a
variation on that theme: "We don't know why we haven't heard
this piece before."

Despite its brevity, I feel both exhilaration and exhaustion
when I give the final cutoff. There are many challenges for the
conductor, but the journey, when finished, always lingers in
the mind and heart for a very long time.

Elgar: Symphony No. 2

Played with some regularity only in Great Britain, this work is
a remarkable excursion that seems to place the composer in
both an urban and a rural environment. Elgar always wore his
nationality on his musical sleeve, but for this piece he seemed
to get away to another place altogether.

It was 1975. The place was Orchestra Hall in Minneapolis, and
this was the new venue's debut season. In February the Chicago
Symphony came to play, with pieces that departed far from the
standard repertoire. Schoenberg's Orchestra Variations was on
the program as well as the Elgar Second. It was as if the administration of the Minnesota Orchestra did not want their own

orchestra to be overshadowed by this most celebrated orchestra under Georg Solti.

I had never heard the Elgar before this encounter. Not only did the Windy City musicians tear the roof off the new building, they converted me into a true believer in the greatness of this work. Sometimes I am asked which of Elgar's two symphonies I prefer. Certainly I love them both, but in terms of actual conducting satisfaction, the clear winner is the Second.

The luxurious orchestration is reminiscent of Richard Strauss, with a few concessions to exotic percussion in the third movement. Like so many composers in the early part of the twentieth century, Elgar had to contend with the newer sounds coming from the likes of Stravinsky and Schoenberg. Like Rachmaninoff, Mahler, and others, Elgar chose to keep his feet firmly planted in the developments of the previous century, never abandoning his penchant for Edwardian Romanticism.

The Second Symphony is not an easy piece to conduct, especially the first movement. One has to keep in mind where material recurs, sustain tension when needed, and relax in certain sections. There is a virtuosity required from the orchestra that is almost unrelenting. Again, the similarity to Strauss is clear. But there are few moments that are more invigorating to conduct than those last few bars in the first movement. If you had a great horn section, which certainly Chicago did, you might feel so completely satisfied with this portion of the symphony that you would just tune out the rest of the work, which of course would be a shame.

There are various subtexts at play in this piece. It has been assumed that the second movement is an elegy to Edward VII, who had just died. There is also the possibility that the music honors other close friends who had passed away. In any event, there is no question that this is framed as a funeral march. Perhaps the most touching moment occurs at the recapitulation of the main theme, but with the addition of an obbligato oboe part, which should be played with great freedom, almost out of rhythm with the rest of the orchestra.

The structure of the third movement combines rondo, scherzo, and trio all in one place. The percussion section has the work's most potent outbursts and at one point almost obliterates the rest of the orchestra. This is also among the most technically challenging works in the repertoire, with notes flying by at the quickest pace one can imagine.

Finales are hard to write for most composers. How to end a work has befuddled many. Elgar's choice here is perfect but is also one of the reasons the piece has not achieved more popularity. It starts with a lovely theme that will undergo several variations. Although it is in sonata form, the composer manages to achieve a seamless flow from one section to the other. There is an unwritten and clearly optional organ pedal part, and this entry leads us into the most sublime of codas. After all the tumult, one feels the sense of loss as the music fades away. It is precisely this quiet conclusion that vexes many in the audience and perhaps turns conductors away from presenting the work.

The symphony, written in 1911, encompasses so much of what the early twentieth century was about. War was on the horizon, people felt unsafe, and music was changing direction, particularly in terms of harmony. Elgar hung on to his past but continued to expand the technical demands on the orchestra. This puts him in line with Mahler, but for me, I find just a bit more depth and passion in Elgar, with the possible exception of Mahler's Ninth Symphony. The Elgar Second is a work I always look forward to conducting.

Shostakovich: Symphony No. 8

This symphony, like some of the other pieces on the list, summarizes a lifetime of struggle. There were still seven others to be written, and numerous other masterpieces, but for me, the Eighth is like nothing else. And yet, in some ways, it is like everything else.

Although the composer did not provide a programmatic description, there is no question that World War II pervades this symphony. In fact, many group the Seventh, Eighth, and Ninth Symphonies of Shostakovich into a "wartime trilogy." The Seventh it is all about the fight, the Eighth reveals the consequences, and in the Ninth the composer exposes the futility of it all.

I don't remember the first time I encountered this work. Most likely it was via a recording, as performances were rare during my student years. When I finally got around to studying the piece, the boldness seemed to jump off the page and into my ears.

In the opening we are reminded of the first few bars of Shostakovich's Fifth Symphony. In fact, much of the structure is determined by the apology given by the composer for having written music "unfriendly" to the state. The Soviets did not take kindly to his earlier dissonant works, and the Fifth became his way of asking for forgiveness. But the difference between these two first movements is that in the Eighth, the level of intensity is ratcheted up in nontriumphant ways. The lengthy English horn solo near the end is as beautiful and sad as one can imagine.

We then come to two contrasting scherzi. The first is slightly jovial but mostly sarcastic. Paying attention to articulation and accents, as well as holding the pulse steady, is key—that, and observing all the little crescendi indicated. The third movement is a relentless machine of devastation.

There is no letup of tension whatsoever, and it all culminates in a huge percussion sound that is ear-shattering as well as emotionally devastating.

From this, we move directly into a passacaglia, but it is so bleak and dark that we are unaware of the formal structure. The entire movement is played at a very soft dynamic—again, Vaughan Williams's Sixth Symphony comes to mind. Eventually the clarinets lead us into the finale.

This movement is the most enigmatic of all, with formality thrown out the window. There are fugal gestures, block-chord dissonances, and playful moments. But for me, it is the coda that is the most indelible moment in the entire symphony. One of the longest-sustained C major chords ever written is played by strings. Various contrasting harmonies play against a three-note pizzicato in the basses. This is easily the most depressing use of a key that is usually reserved for joy and happiness.

No one should be unmoved by the time the hour passes. And I am drained.

Strauss: *An Alpine Symphony*

This is a piece that many people hate, perhaps even more than Strauss's *Symphonia Domestica*. Critics are put off by the programmatic nature of the work, and audiences do not know what to make of the mountain journey and its enigmatic conclusion. And yet, there is no other work like this in the symphonic repertoire.

Yes, it is an orchestral indulgence: in terms of sheer size, Strauss's original instrumentation outranks anything by Mahler. The offstage brass, who play for just a little more than thirty seconds, can be a budget breaker for artistic administrators. Add a large percussion section and an organ and mix in boatloads of notes and the soft ending, and—well, you get the idea.

This is the last purely orchestral work Strauss would write. After *An Alpine Symphony*, he would devote the rest of his life to composing operas, songs, and works with solo instruments. Coming about eleven years after the *Symphonia Domestica*, another large-scale piece, the *Alpine Symphony* enjoyed a much-anticipated first performance. Alas, the public and press seemed not to understand what the composer was trying to achieve, and it looked like the work would be relegated to the curiosity shelf. Strauss, however, believed it to be his finest orchestral work.

An Alpine Symphony had a comeback when sonic developments improved to the point where home listeners could use this splendorous music to test-drive their home audio systems. And it was the first piece of classical music to be issued on CD. I suspect this is how many listeners encountered the work for the first time.

For me, this work represents the pinnacle of Strauss's mastery of orchestral forces. One can argue for or against the programmatic nature of the piece, but it is impossible to deny the sheer brilliance of its scoring. Whether one considers the fifty-minute journey to be actual, metaphorical, or philosophical, it is an incredible display of virtuosity, perhaps unmatched by any other composer.

Strauss remained firmly entrenched in the aesthetic of nineteenth-century Romanticism, but here he utilizes the orchestral forces that were unleashed by both Wagner and Stravinsky. *An Alpine Symphony* even moves into the realm of postchromaticism, with the descending scale becoming a chord cluster, foreshadowing Ligeti. The development of the various musical themes, including a reference back to Strauss's *Also sprach Zarathustra*, gives the symphony a truly personal as well as worldly view of the mountains we must all seek to scale.

Along the way we get hunting horns, cowbells, waterfalls, missteps, and the eventual reaching of the summit. It is here that the work takes a reflective tone, almost religious in its melodies and harmonies. An elegy reminds us of those who did not survive the trek. Little drops of rain pelt us on our rapid descent, accompanied by thunder, lightning, and a roaring wind machine. Over the next six minutes we will retrace the entire trip.

And just when you believe that it is not possible to throw something new into the mixture, Strauss gives us that Ligeti-like chord, puts in a couple of bars of violin phrases, and then has the violins do a lengthy descending glissando, one of the most heartbreaking gestures I know.

As with almost every masterpiece, maintaining structure, being flexible with tempi, and letting the orchestra find its collective voice is imperative in *An Alpine Symphony*. Perhaps it is a work more enjoyed by the members of the orchestra than the audience. But when an outstanding performance of the *Alpine* is heard, it is unforgettable to all.

Rachmaninoff: *Rhapsody on a Theme of Paganini*

You might think the inclusion of a work with a soloist is unfair. After all, much of the success of such a piece depends on who is in the spotlight. But in this case, the role of the orchestra is as significant as that of the piano. Even more to the point for me, the *Rhapsody* epitomizes sheer perfection as a composition and provides the ultimate in challenges for the conductor.

Up until Brahms, works for soloist and orchestra were usually meant as showcase pieces for the featured artist. Certainly there was a great deal of interplay between the protagonist and the ensemble, as evidenced by Mozart and Beethoven, but the overwhelming majority of pieces titled "concerto" were meant to display the solo instrument.

As the nineteenth century moved to its close, the interweaving of the various components began to change. And in 1934 Rachmaninoff best exemplified the changed relationship of soloist and orchestra with his *Rhapsody*. There are no true cadenzas or even lengthy tuttis. Like the finale of Beethoven's Third Symphony, this piece is really a set of variations. And as in the "Eroica," the theme does not appear immediately.

The Paganini Caprice on which it is based remains a staple of the violin repertoire, and many composers have utilized this tune in one way or another. Rachmaninoff's is easily the most expansive and shows the virtuosity of both soloist and orchestra. The pianist and orchestra alternate taking the lead.

When you get to the famous Eighteenth Variation, the one where the melody is turned upside down, it is the pianist's turn to set not only the tempo but also the mood. Upon the entrance of the orchestra, the conductor must maintain the same degree of flexibility while the soloist fits in cascades of chords. Pianist and orchestra play off of each other, and by the time the piano quietly finishes, it is almost as if time has been suspended throughout the entire section.

That is what makes this work such a delight to conduct. The give-and-take element must be mutual, and much can be left to the moment of performance. My own favorite collaborations have been the ones where unpredictability reigns. That doesn't mean that chaos ensues, but rather that a true feeling of spontaneity is achieved. By the time the last few notes are sounded, with the clear intent of humor, soloist and conductor can only wink at each other—if the chemistry has produced the desired result.

PART TWO

SIX OF THE BEST

Friendship . . . is not something you learn in school. But if you haven't learned the meaning of friendship, you really haven't learned anything.

—Muhammad Ali

EUGENE ORMANDY

Let me explain what I do here. I don't want to confuse you
any more than absolutely necessary.

The annals of music are rife with names that are unfamiliar
to succeeding generations. Today, the mention of such
conductors as William Steinberg, Charles Munch, Rafael
Kubelik, Erich Leinsdorf, and Rodzínski elicit blank stares from
most musicians under forty years of age. In some cases (though
not those above) the obscurity is probably deserved, but in my

mind there is one conductor who remains perhaps the most underappreciated of all.

Born in 1899, Eugene Ormandy came to the attention of the impresario Arthur Judson, who arranged for the Hungarian to visit the United States in 1931, at age thirty-two, as a substitute for the ailing Toscanini. The success of this engagement led to Ormandy's being offered the music directorship of the Minneapolis Symphony Orchestra. After five years and many highly lauded recordings, Ormandy went to Philadelphia and assumed the role previously held by Leopold Stokowski.

For forty-four years Ormandy led this fabled ensemble and maintained the sonority, personality, and individuality of the orchestra. The so-called Philadelphia sound became a catch-phrase, though it was later renounced by Ormandy's successor, Riccardo Muti, who said an orchestra should only reflect the sound of the composer.

Ormandy's preference was the very opposite. He favored a lush, cushy sonority for the orchestra regardless of what it was playing. In a way, he was emulating the great soloists of the time, whose characteristics were distinctive and individual throughout a recital of varied works.

One thing was certain: it was almost impossible to hear a bad performance under Ormandy's direction. It may not have been earthshaking, but it always reflected a high degree of music making.

Sneaking into Carnegie Hall was not too difficult during my student years in New York. And since I knew a couple of people in the Philadelphia Orchestra, they got me into not only the concerts but the rehearsals as well. On one occasion I introduced myself to Ormandy, who was surprised at my interest in the orchestra. He told me that I should feel free to come to Philadelphia anytime and offered to arrange tickets for the concerts.

In 1967 the Philadelphia Orchestra made its first trip to Japan. One of the cellists refused to go because he was afraid of flying. My mother got an invitation to fill in, as she was very good friends with the first cellist, Samuel Mayes. She told a story of the first rehearsal:

> I was seated at the back of the section, something I was not used to. Ormandy came out, and we began with the Beethoven Seventh. Now you have to understand that working in the Hollywood studios required that the musicians be very precise when it came to coordinating the sound with the picture. In order to do this, one had to play exactly with the conductor's beat. Ormandy was not exactly clear, and in general, the orchestra seemed to play just a fraction behind what he was conducting. So he gave this sweeping gesture to start the first movement, and I came crashing in ahead of everyone else. The orchestra laughed, and my stand partner said that I would figure it out quickly.

Eventually, my mother would donate my father's violin, a Guarnerius, one of the del Gesù family, to the Philadelphia Orchestra. It became known as the Spalding del Gesù, as Albert

Spalding was the previous musician who owned it. Among other pieces, the Barber Violin Concerto was premiered on this instrument. On one of my trips to Philadelphia the concert-master, Norman Carol, played the work on the same instrument used in the premiere. It was also the violin that I heard my father play a couple of days before he died.

At Carnegie Hall, after a performance of the Beethoven Second Symphony, I went back to Ormandy's dressing room. He had shut his door but allowed me to come in nevertheless. He said, "If you ever give a performance that was as poor as the one we just did, you will need to stop conducting." I did not think it was horrible at all but decided not to say anything.

There followed a series of letters between Ormandy and my agent, Mariedi Anders. The San Francisco–based Anders was related to the maestro's wife, and as a manager she was as assertive as anyone I have ever met. Eventually, in 1975, Ormandy invited me to conduct his orchestra. It was a dream come true.

Ormandy himself introduced me to the orchestra. It is very rare that the music director is around when guests appear, but Ormandy was devoted to his ensemble and did not do much guest conducting. Perhaps that is why the sound of the orchestra was so consistent.

Although his English was good, several of his odd locutions became legendary. They were kept in a diary by one of the orchestra musicians and included:

"Why do you always insist on playing while I'm trying to conduct?"

"With us tonight is William Warfield, who is with us tonight. He is a wonderful man, and so is his wife."

"I told him he'd have a heart attack a year ago, but unfortunately he lived a year longer."

"During the rests—pray."

"That's the way Stravinsky was. Bup, bup, bup, bup. The poor guy's dead now. Play it legato."

There were many in the orchestra who were openly pleased when the maestro announced that he was stepping down as music director. After many years with Ormandy at the helm, they wanted a different point of view. But within a few years the majority realized that the former boss was unique and contributed true individuality to the Philadelphia Orchestra.

As mentioned, Ormandy did little guest conducting, but I remember going to hear him with the Chicago Symphony when he was perhaps not at the height of his powers. Nonetheless, after ten minutes, without saying a word, he had that orchestra sounding very much like his Philadelphians. As with so many great conductors, one could not readily figure out why that was so. He just radiated the sound he wanted and got the results he required.

In addition to his mastery of tonal splendor, Ormandy was one of the greatest collaborators with soloists. Somehow, his beat patterns changed when he was working with pianists, violinists, and others positioned at the front of the stage. All of a sudden, clarity became the watchword, and virtually every artist I know loved playing with him.

In these days of international similarity amongst symphony orchestras, it is with a degree of fondness and sadness that I look back at what Ormandy accomplished. The Philadelphia sound will always be linked to their longtime music director, and more than likely we will not hear this type of individuality again. Perhaps the maestro said it best: "This is a very democratic organization, so let's take a vote. All those who disagree with me, raise your hands!"

NATHAN MILSTEIN

At that time, I did not really like violin playing.

Growing up in a household filled with Russian émigrés, my brother and I were constantly reminded of the glories that were the motherland's distinguished school of music teaching. It seemed as if the Germans and French, not to mention the Americans, did not exist. But if my parents spoke of one artist with special reverence, it was the violinist Nathan Milstein. Not even Horowitz or Heifetz was held in such high esteem.

When I found out that Milstein was available to be the soloist on one of my programs with the St. Louis Symphony, I was overjoyed but filled with anxiety. Like so many musicians from Russia, he had a reputation for an explosive temperament and a downright mean spirit. I don't think there is anyone who encountered Milstein who does not have at least one great anecdote about his personality.

Here is mine.

It was December of 1974, and Milstein was seventy years old. During this birthday season, he was making the rounds to various orchestras, playing one of his signature pieces, the Brahms Violin Concerto.

The week before he was to appear with us, Milstein was in Los Angeles with Zubin Mehta. Usually, with a piece like this, only one rehearsal with the soloist is needed. A fine orchestra knows the work inside out and can quickly detect any nuance the soloist brings to the piece. Zubin felt that meeting with Nathan before the orchestra rehearsal was not necessary, and so when Milstein came to the stage—having requested and having been denied a one-on-one with the conductor—he started right in.

The concerto opens with an orchestral tutti of about three minutes before the violin plays a single note. One bar after Milstein's entrance, he turned to the orchestra and said something like, "You know, in the sixth bar, the note is not being held long enough." Now Mehta had to go all the way back to the beginning of the piece and play through that section, with Milstein stopping him throughout to correct what he thought were inaccuracies. It was all baiting, just to get back at Zubin for not agreeing to a meeting. Nathan managed to eat up almost the whole rehearsal, leaving very little time for the orchestra to play the other works on the program.

I was determined not to let that happen, and upon Milstein's arrival in St. Louis I left messages for him with the driver, symphony staff, and hotel saying that I would like to discuss the Brahms that night before the orchestra session the next morning.

At 7:00 I showed up at the Chase Park Plaza, the grand hotel in St. Louis. I went up to Milstein's floor and from the hallway could hear him practicing. But something was amiss. The pieces he was playing were all a half tone lower than usual. I knocked and he opened the door, violin in hand. I could not help but notice that he had a practice mute on the instrument, one that barely allows the musician to be heard. After exchanging greetings— we had never met—I asked him why he practiced with the strings tuned down. He said that it was better for the violin, as there was less pressure on the bridge of the instrument.

For about an hour he talked, without playing a note. And what he wanted to tell me was how horrible all conductors were. Toscanini, Walter, Stokowski, Fritz Reiner—all of them. Stories of their incompetence rolled out of his mouth as if on a conveyor belt. This did not instill a lot of confidence in me.

Finally I asked if we could go over some places in the concerto. He said, "Why? I know it, you know it, and the orchestra knows it. Let's just do it tomorrow when we are all together."

I was having none of that, knowing what had happened in Los Angeles the week before. He eventually played a few passages, but I was on to him. Growing up in an extremely flexible musical environment, I knew that virtually nothing of what he was demonstrating would occur the same way at rehearsal or during the concert.

At the rehearsal, things seemed to be going well. He did not stop me after the first tutti, and we played most of the first movement without pause. Except for the one time I did what he hated most: I turned away and looked at the cello section instead of the soloist. At that moment Milstein started bending the phrase in a direction I was not expecting, and for an instant the ensemble was not together. He stopped us, and the tension set in. From that point, I do not think I ever looked at the orchestra again.

He would say one thing and do another. "No ritard in the last two bars," he warned, and then he added one, yelling at us to watch him. He would purposely rush a passage just to see if I could keep up. But whatever he did, it was never unmusical.

At the first performance, things were going along smoothly, and then, in the last movement, he had a brief memory lapse. The mistake didn't disrupt the concert and we just kept going, but it was clear that he was upset. As we left the stage, he said, loud enough for some of the musicians to hear, "Orchestra play like pigs."

I was devastated.

The audience was rapturous in its ovation. However, I did not want to go back onstage and share a bow with him. Milstein said, "You must behave like professional," and out we went together. Inside, I was a wreck.

John Edwards, the executive director of the Chicago Symphony Orchestra, and my mother had flown in from Chicago to hear this concert. With Milstein, the four of us headed to Tony's, the great St. Louis restaurant. During the ten-minute drive my mother, who had known Nathan through her Russian musical connections, mentioned that she had been doing some television work. Milstein wanted to know which shows she did. *Dallas.*

All of a sudden he lit up and started recapping every episode he could think of. It was his favorite, and now my mother was his idol. The rest of the evening, while I was hoping to be regaled with tales of musical life in Moscow, Vienna, and Paris, the conversation was reduced to a discussion of Southfork.

The second performance was the next evening. Waiting backstage for the concert to begin, and still distraught over Milstein's reaction the night before, I did not say a word to him.

He came up to me, put his arm on my shoulder and said, "You must forgive a foolish old man. It was my fault, not yours. Let's make music."

After that, we performed together several times over the years, always the Brahms. And he simply could not stop his childlike musical pranks. But I loved him and cherished those times dearly.

JOHN BROWNING

Music is what we can't say with words. In many cases it goes deeper than words; it's a philosophy, it's a religion, it's the human experience.

It must have been Tyler's fault. The little papillon traveled the world, sat on the great stages, and became John Browning's best friend. When others might have pulled out pictures of their children, John would open a little bag to reveal the five-pound beast. Maybe that is why we got thrown out of a restaurant in Minneapolis.

I never heard John raise his voice. He certainly complained enough, but anger just was not in his repertoire. As one of an extraordinary generation of American pianists, John really did not grab the public's attention to the extent that Leon Fleisher, Gary Graffman, Byron Janis, or Van Cliburn did. But his gifts were just as commanding. Of all those keyboard giants, John Browning was the elegant one. There was just a touch of Fred Astaire in him, and he could almost have come out of a Noel Coward play.

Born in Denver in 1933, John was accepted into the Juilliard School at the age of ten, studying with the legendary Rosina Lhévinne. Eventually his family moved to Los Angeles, but John still liked to speak of his mountain roots. I heard him play several times both in downtown Los Angeles and at the Hollywood Bowl; however, I didn't meet him until I arrived in St. Louis as the assistant conductor. From that time in 1969 until his untimely death in 2003 at the age of sixty-nine, we were the closest of friends as well as collaborators.

Openly gay, John never seemed to be uncomfortable with his sexuality. He spoke of lovers and one-night stands. His sense of humor was particularly notable for its bawdiness. One morning in a Minneapolis hotel, I was waiting for him by the elevators in the lobby. When the doors opened, there was John with this big grin, telling the world, "I got laid last night!"

His repertoire was very broad, but he is best remembered for his musical relationship with Samuel Barber. In 1962 John gave the world premiere of the Barber Piano Concerto, written for him and presented at the opening concerts at Lincoln Center. He must have played it more than five hundred times, and always made it sound fresh, as if each performance were the first.

In 1991, almost thirty years after the premiere and first recording, John chose to redo the Barber with me in St. Louis. It is not very often that a musician gets to work with the person who was in on the creation of a masterpiece, and I was more than grateful for the opportunity.

We played the concerto together in Tokyo, Amsterdam, New York, and half a dozen other cities. The St. Louis recording sessions were a delight, especially when John was trying to figure out, with the recording engineer, how to achieve the ideal sound balance between piano and orchestra. After a few takes John was still not satisfied. The technician, William Hoekstra, went down to the musicians' lounge, absconded with a pool cue, and used it as the stick to make the lid of the piano higher. It worked, and we won a Grammy.

By this time Tyler was inseparable from John, who never went anywhere without the dog. Sometimes John would place Tyler's carrier beside the piano, and the dog would stay quietly inside, enjoying the music. Once, on a visit to Blossom Music Center—the Cleveland Orchestra's summer home—with the St. Louis Symphony, John brought the dog onstage during one of his bows. I suspect the audience forgot about everything else on the program that night.

One time in Minnesota John played the Barber Sonata at 7:00 in the evening and returned to the stage an hour later to play the same composer's piano concerto. It was an unforgettable feat.

In Saratoga, the summer home of the Philadelphia Orchestra, we were scheduled to perform Prokofiev's Third Piano Concerto, a work we had often done together. When we arrived for rehearsal, we were informed that everyone was expecting the Second Concerto. Even John could not work up that prodigiously virtuosic piece in just a few minutes. As is the case with many al fresco concerts, there was only one rehearsal. We asked if we could get a set of parts for the Third Piano Concerto in time for the evening performance.

"But there will be no time to rehearse it," an official declared.

John replied, "I know the piece, Leonard knows the piece, and the orchestra knows the piece. We can sight-read it at the concert." That is exactly what we did. It was one of the finest performances I can remember.

On a clear Friday morning in January 2003, my telephone rang at home. It was John, calling to say that he had exorcised his demons. Tyler had been dead for not quite a year. The call came from his home in Sister Bay, Wisconsin. I knew that John had been ill for about six months, but I did not realize the extent of his malady. Four days later, on January 26, John joined Tyler.

I miss him tremendously, but I know that he is somewhere making rude remarks to St. Peter. Tyler is quietly looking on.

ISAAC STERN

Photo by © Hulton-Deutsch Collection/Corbis/Corbis via Getty Images

*I have a responsibility to pass on to the next generation
what I learned from my teachers. . . . It keeps me young
and reminds me where I came from.*

During the course of my conducting life it has been my
good fortune to know many distinguished artists. Some
have been more than helpful, and high up on that list
was Isaac Stern. Of course, there are countless people who
could make that statement.

In 1980 Isaac celebrated his sixtieth birthday. We had worked together several times and seemed to have a great musical, as well as personal, rapport. He invited me to be part of his celebratory season (which lasted about two and a half years) in conjunction with a project he was doing in Paris. He said that he wanted the French to "understand music." That was his first mistake.

Isaac would spend almost four months playing eight concerti and numerous pieces of chamber music with French musicians. Six of the programs were with orchestras, and I conducted two of these. This was my debut in the City of Lights. My high school French was minimal at best. Stern was fluent but retained his distinctly American accent and inflection.

The first program consisted of Verdi's *Sicilian Vespers* Overture, the Brahms Double Concerto with the principal cellist of the Orchestre National de France, and Bartók's Violin Concerto No. 2. At the first rehearsal, and indeed all of them, Isaac sat beside me and offered comments to the orchestra as we went along. He introduced me to the ensemble and told me to start with the Verdi.

I could not help but notice that the first bassoon was sitting about fifteen feet away from the first clarinet, but I said nothing at the time. Usually they were right next to each other. After we played through the piece, I mentioned this to Isaac. He said something to the woodwinds, and all hell broke loose. Commotion ensued and arguments flew around the rehearsal studio. Isaac said we should take an intermission. This was only ten minutes into the session.

The following is a summation of the discussion that took place near the podium with the bassoon section and lasted almost twenty minutes.

Stern: "Why are you sitting so far from the clarinets?"

Bassoonist: "If I sit next to them, the trumpets are blasting into my ears."

Slatkin: "Can we move the brass so the horns are behind the woodwinds and the trumpets and trombones are off to the right?"

Bassoonist: "That is a fine idea. It is how we usually sit."

Stern: "Then why didn't you start the rehearsal in that position?"

Bassoonist: "Because we did not know how you would like us to sit!"

This is how the whole week went. Not a day passed when there was not some incident of this sort. And it all culminated on the day of the concert.

Our hotel was a grand total of two blocks from the Théâtre des Champs-Élysées, where the concert took place. Isaac and I agreed to meet in the lobby thirty minutes before the show and walk down to the hall. Earlier in the day we were told that the pope would be in Paris that afternoon and there was a parade scheduled down avenue Montaigne, the same street as the performance venue. It was requested that our concert begin at 8:00 and not 7:30 as advertised, to make sure that everyone could get in.

So, half an hour before curtain time, we walked down the street, made two rights, and got to the stage door, where the administration of the orchestra was waiting; they were clearly upset.

"Where have you been?" one of them inquired.

"We were at the hotel. Is there a problem?"

"The audience is here. The radio is starting its transmission."

"But you said the concert would start at 8:00 because of the pope's visit."

"Yes, but the parade was canceled. We must start."

"Then why didn't you call to tell us?"

"Because we did not want to disturb you!"

Isaac turned the brightest shade of red I have ever seen. How he got through the demanding program I will never know, but it was clear that he was not focused on the music, although he played brilliantly. During the applause for the Bartók, he said that I should go wait in the dressing room, as he had a few words he wanted to say to the audience. Of course, I stayed in the wings to hear what he had to say (my French was not *that* bad).

"Ladies and gentlemen, I want to thank you all for coming here this evening. I did not realize that there were so many Jews left in Paris!"

That was when I went back to the dressing room.

After the performance, we went to a lovely restaurant across the street from our hotel. Joining in the party were Isaac's family as well as Vladimir Horowitz and Madame Prokofiev, among others. Since that time I have had a wonderful relationship with French musicians, food, and wine.

Isaac was a constant supporter and advisor to me for many years. As with many great artists, he sometimes did not heed his own advice. More than likely he should have stopped playing the violin a bit earlier, and he most certainly should have spent more time practicing. But that was Isaac, sitting in his hotel room, violin in one hand, telephone in the other, watching tennis on television. He used to be referred to as "the American Heifetz," a moniker that no one could possibly have lived up to, but the greatness that emanated from Isaac's hands was felt by everyone fortunate enough to have heard him.

He could speak as well as anyone on the lecture circuit. Often called upon to say a few words, he would have memorized the names of everyone in attendance. Devoted to music, arts-related causes, Israel, food, and wine, Isaac enjoyed life to the fullest. He was the man who saved Carnegie Hall; premiered works by Bernstein, Schuman, Krzysztof Penderecki and Henri Dutilleux; and ran with the most important figures in the world.

Isaac may have had his faults, but there was no better advocate on the planet for what was just and right. We all lost an important musical ambassador when he died.

GILBERT KAPLAN

*It's like a love affair, and like all good love affairs, it
continues to grow. I even have the approval of my wife.*

There is obsession and there is passion. Many times the
two together produce horrific results, but once in a while
something extraordinary comes out of this relationship.

In 1981 I received a call from Gilbert Kaplan, founder of the
publication *Institutional Investor*. He wanted to speak to me about
Gustav Mahler's Second Symphony. Gil had seen that I was to

conduct the work in Denver in a few months and wondered if he could observe the rehearsals and concerts.

Oh, and he also wanted to know how to conduct the piece.

The fact that he had no professional training as a conductor, or even as a musician, sent up red flags immediately. But as Kaplan continued to talk, I became intrigued by the audacity of what he was attempting. Up to this point I had not done much teaching, but the Mahler Second was now in my repertoire, and I felt that seeing him was the least I could do.

The somewhat balding, almost professorial-looking man who came to my dressing room prior to the first rehearsal was hardly the imposing personality one usually associates with the podium. Soft-spoken and direct, he explained that this one work had intrigued him for many years, and that he had done a great deal of research in an effort to unlock the secrets Mahler had left for us. But studying it is one thing; conducting it is another matter altogether.

I asked him if he could read a score. Gil said he could not, but that as a child he played piano and had a thorough concept of the Second Symphony. So I treated him as I would a student in the first year of a conducting class. We went through beat patterns, worked on independence of the left hand, practiced his posture on the podium, and so on. The Mahler did not enter into the discussion until the third day in Denver.

It was time to see if it was possible for an amateur to direct one of the largest pieces in the entire repertoire. We worked tirelessly, and over the course of the week I ended up spending more time with Gil than I did with the orchestra, soloists, and chorus for the performances.

There was no question that he knew the piece inside out. He even made some corrections in the timpani part in my score. It was just a question of giving him the technique to accomplish what for most people might have seemed impossible. When my concerts concluded and we had to leave Denver, I told him that although there was still a lot of work to do, I believed that he could lead a competent performance of it. He was also studying with other teachers and conductors, who would hopefully give him the continued encouragement to work toward his eventual goal of presenting Mahler's Second at a public concert.

Gil most certainly had his detractors. Many of the leading conductors in the world refused to see him, and many openly disparaged such an undertaking. My own thoughts were more philosophical than musical. It is my opinion that one of the most misused words in the English language is "amateur." To pursue one's passion, with no hint of personal gain, is to be admired, not admonished. Gil stood as an exemplar of how to turn an obsession into something wonderful.

In 1982, at Avery Fisher Hall no less, Gil stood in front of the American Symphony Orchestra and Westminster Choir, fulfilling his dream. Prior to the performance he told the audience that he did not know if this would be an ideal account of the Mahler Second, but he promised these invited guests a fabulous dinner afterward. Critics were not asked to attend, but one did, Leighton Kerner of the *Village Voice*, and he praised the presentation as "revelatory." From that point on the musical world started to pay attention to the financial wizard who became a conductor.

Gil sold his magazine in 1984 for an estimated $75 million, which enabled him to devote the majority of his time to continued Mahler research. He bought the original manuscript of the Second Symphony as well as other related Mahleriana. He also established a foundation, giving the public access to a wealth of material on Mahler's work. And he conducted more than a hundred performances of the Mahler Second around the world.

At my invitation, he led the piece in both St. Louis and Washington. There were mixed feelings among those two orchestras, but the musicians eventually realized that they were in the presence of someone who knew the work as well as anyone and could verbalize his concepts clearly.

In 2008 Gil led the New York Philharmonic. The *New York Times* reported:

> His efforts were evident throughout a performance of sharp definition and shattering power. From the acute punch of the opening notes, every detail of this huge, complex score came through with unusual clarity and impeccable balance. Every gesture had purpose and impact, and the performance as a whole had an inexorable sweep. . . . It seems likely that no one is better equipped to reveal the impact of precisely what Mahler put on the page.

However, a member of the orchestra wrote a piece for the same paper that to me seemed petty, especially considering that

Gil received no conductor's fee and provided funding for the extra musicians, soloists, and chorus. This is a bit of what a trombonist wrote:

> Much has been written about Mr. Kaplan's passion for Mahler's great symphony as if this emotion is unique to him. This assertion is an insult to all professional musicians who have dedicated their entire lives and have sacrificed much toward the preservation of all the great works of history's finest composers. His continued appearances are also an affront to all "real" conductors who have toiled relentlessly for the recognition they duly deserve.

It hurt Gil deeply. He was asked repeatedly to perform the work after this missive, and he did so, but perhaps with a bit of a heavy heart.

We became very close friends. His wife, Lena, and their four children are not only brilliant, but also warm. Gil was the epitome of generosity and treated me as if I were a member of his family. He taught classes at the Juilliard School and gave lectures about Mahler, both the man and his music. I asked him to do so in Detroit and Lyon.

Gil was scheduled to lecture on the Second Symphony once again in the Motor City on the occasion of my first performance of the work with the DSO in December 2015. He called me a few weeks before the event to say that he had been diagnosed with cancer and was undergoing experimental treatments. He did not think the doctors would let him travel.

In his place his assistant, Heidi Bryson, delivered the talk. Before she began reading Gil's script, she read a letter from him. At the end Heidi handed me a baton, one used by Mahler himself in performances of the Second Symphony. Gil had said it was time that this baton be passed along. I knew then that the end was near.

Gil Kaplan died just a few minutes after midnight on New Year's Day, 2016. The loss was felt like one of the hammer blows in Mahler's Sixth Symphony. A few months later a memorial took place in Zankel Hall at Carnegie. I was on the road and could not attend, but I sent a video to honor his memory. At the end I spoke six words, which will remain true forever.

"*Ewig* [forever], my friend. *Ewig, our* friend."

JOHN WILLIAMS

There is more music to be found in poetry and in the quiet contemplation of nature, than in studying music itself.

In 2004 John was among the five honorees of the Kennedy Center in Washington. Most people know about the show, which is televised annually, but the real highlight of the week is a dinner the night before, hosted by the Secretary of State—Condoleezza Rice at the time. I was asked to deliver the toast.

How can one describe this man and his accomplishments in two minutes? His quiet demeanor is at odds with a great deal of the music he has written. Over the years John has distinguished himself with virtually every award possible. The recipient of Emmys, Oscars, Grammys, and honorary degrees, he must need an entire building to store his trophies.

I first met John when I was a young boy in Los Angeles. Like so many other musicians on the West Coast, he began his professional life in the studios. John's piano skills were extraordinary, and those who heard him play can attest to his artistry. Quickly moving up the ladder of success, he ventured into television with memorable scores for shows such as *Lost in Space*, *Voyage to the Bottom of the Sea*, and *NBC Nightly News*. He has written scores for four Olympic games as well as a presidential inauguration. We won't even talk about the movies.

Not unlike Leonard Bernstein, John has made an important mark—but one mentioned less frequently—in his works for the concert hall. His concerti in particular are played often. It is possible to assume that these works are programmed for his name recognition, but audiences expecting to hear the sounds of *Star Wars* are quite surprised. He can be edgy, as in the Flute Concerto, or picturesque, as with the Horn Concerto, or simply virtuosic, as exemplified by the First Violin Concerto.

He established a new dynamic in his role as conductor of the Boston Pops. It was a hotly debated choice—John Williams as successor to Arthur Fiedler! But John's classical background, coupled with his eminence as a composer of film music, made him the perfect candidate. He brought a fresh repertoire to his concerts and became an iconic personality whom other conductors envied.

In 2003 I invited John to co-direct a two-week festival in Washington. It was called, appropriately, "Soundtracks," and during the six concerts we presented everything centered on film music as an integral part of the concertgoing experience. John argued that if Wagner or Puccini had lived well into the twentieth century, they would have embraced the medium. He'll get no argument from me.

At one of the performances John and I sat at an upright, wearing visors like the piano players for the silent films. He had written a five-minute piece that we played while a montage of clips was shown onscreen. I do not know if I have ever had a better time as a pianist. During the final concert John explained to the audience how music is put together with film. After demonstrating devices such as streamers, click tracks, and punch marks, he showed part of the third *Indiana Jones* movie, without music. Then, with headsets on, the National Symphony proceeded to astound everyone with a precisely timed, live sound track that had listeners panting for breath and experiencing firsthand how the magic is created.

In addition, John is quite a raconteur. And with so many experiences, there are stories to be told. He regaled the NSO audience with a story about my mother.

As was the case for so many Hollywood composers, John regarded my mother as his first choice of cellist. In the mid-1970s a little thriller was made called *Jaws*, one of the earliest collaborations between John and Steven Spielberg. Is it possible that this relationship rivals that of Mozart and Da Ponte, or Verdi and Boito, perhaps even Rodgers and Hammerstein?

Noticing that I was in the audience, John said, "Your mother has been scaring people silly since 1975."

From the balcony I shouted back, "She was scaring them long before that!"

And so I had to come up with something very special for that pre–Kennedy Center Honors dinner at the State Department.

Here is what I said:

"Most people think that Beethoven wrote the most familiar music using just four notes." Then I intoned, "DA-DA-DA-DUUUUM," trying to voice the opening of the Fifth Symphony.

"But John has him beat by two notes," I stated. Then I sang, "DAAAA-DUM!" in imitation of the shark motive from *Jaws*.

Everyone laughed, but all I cared about was how John reacted. His smile and hug a few minutes later were all I could ever want. To have known him for all these years has been a true privilege.

INTERLUDE ONE

———

THE MIND WANDERS

There are times when thinking about something is the worst possible policy.

———John Christopher, *When the Tripods Came*

The beginning of a concert has an accompanying ritual that varies from place to place. In the United States, usually the concertmaster enters after the orchestra is already seated, takes a solo bow, and then signals for the oboe to sound the A.

In most of Europe, however, the entire orchestra is offstage until about a minute before the concert is supposed to start. Then they enter en masse. The audience applauds until the last few stragglers make it to their stands, and finally the concertmaster makes a separate entrance and tunes the orchestra.

Much the same occurs with the British orchestras, but there is one big difference. When the orchestra is in place onstage, the assistant concertmaster tunes the orchestra, and then the concertmaster enters to a second round of applause, bows, and sits down. To top it all off, the conductor enters and shakes the concertmaster's hand as if they were seeing each other for the first time, when in fact they were together just moments before in the backstage area.

These preconcert rituals are part of what audiences have come to expect; however, they seem a bit dated to me. My own preference is that the entire orchestra be onstage, including the concertmaster. The conductor enters, the orchestra rises, and everyone shares in the applause. It is simple and elegant and yet retains some of the traditions everyone is used to.

The pianos in the two main concert halls in Vienna are tuned to A = 443. In my lifetime I have seen the frequency creep up three points. According to scholars, this puts the A more than a full tone higher from where it was a couple of centuries ago.

This produces an overly bright sound due to the tension on the piano strings. Oboists have to make major adjustments to play that high. The pressure of the strings on a violin bridge creates tension that often results in a pinched sound. Most of all, singers have a much more difficult time reaching the high notes.

Be practical here, Vienna. Bring the pitch down to A = 440.

Have you noticed that almost all of the announcements made before a concert begins tend to emphasize the negative? We are told to refrain from taking photos, to silence cell phones, to turn off recording devices, and so on. I keep waiting for seat-belt instructions.

Accidents happen, and they always will. But if we are going to inform the public, let's do it in a more pleasant manner. The Verdi Orchestra in Milan plays a recording of "Spring" from Vivaldi's *The Four Seasons*. About three bars in, a mobile phone rings. Nothing else needs to be said.

The Amsterdam Concertgebouw has a placard showing a cell phone with an X through it. The audience sees it the second they walk in the hall. Again, no words are necessary.

On a tour to Florida with the Detroit Symphony, I actually told the audience, at the conclusion of the program, that they should turn their devices on and feel free to record the encore and take pictures to share with others. The ploy drew a few criticisms, but most patrons felt grateful for the opportunity to take home a concert souvenir.

These announcements will not prevent audio or video piracy. Someone will always find a workaround for virtually any rule or ban. If we must remind the public, let's do it without undue negativity.

Stop reinventing the orchestra! Yes, we do need to examine how we relate to an ever-changing society, but wholesale revolution is not the answer. There will always be people who welcome certain rituals that come with the concert experience.

Those onstage can dress in something other than ultra-formal attire, but casual dress takes away something special. People come for the visual as well as the aural stimulation. A nice, uniform look amongst the musicians is appreciated.

Programming formats for the concerts can be adjusted for various events, but I think that even fifty years from now the majority of concerts will be structured quite similarly to those of the twentieth century. There doesn't always have to be an overture, a concerto, and a symphony, but in most cases this programming formula and its variants will continue to work quite well.

If there is one area that warrants change, it is in efforts to reach a wider audience. But we must remember that, for the most part, the music that we play only appeals to a small segment of the population. Any expansion of that audience is best achieved through education.

Change is good, but tradition continues to have its place.

We all know when a concert begins, but how many of you actually know when it ends?

The answer to this depends on the language of the contract. Many orchestras have adopted a rule that I consider to be a miscarriage of justice. You would think that the simple answer to the question is, "It is over when the applause stops." And that is how I feel as well.

However, many orchestras take the view that since the concertmaster signals the beginning of the event, the departure of that musician should likewise indicate when it is finished. Actually, almost everything is determined by the clock. Most orchestras have a two-hour-and-fifteen-minute performance time limit that begins with the entrance of the concertmaster.

From that point, the clock starts ticking. This means that no matter how prolonged the music or its reception, the concert ends when the little hand hits that point.

We certainly know the approximate length of each piece. It is the intangible that is unknown. What if the soloist plays an encore on his or her own? Should that be counted, as the orchestra sits onstage but does not play? And what happens if the audience is so enthusiastic that the applause runs over the time limit?

I have been told way too often, after coming offstage, that the orchestra must be brought off as well in order to avoid paying overtime.

Really? Depriving the public of its opportunity to show approval of what has been accomplished seems petty and foolish to me. The concert should end when the public decides it is over.

Never underestimate your public.

Once I was conducting a pension-fund concert in Los Angeles but had to get back to St. Louis for a rehearsal the next morning. This meant taking the redeye flight, arriving about 8:00 in the morning and going directly to Powell Hall.

The Los Angeles Philharmonic had graciously given me a first-class ticket so I would be able to sleep a bit more comfortably. A few minutes after I sat down, eight of the largest men I had ever seen entered the cabin, and one was seated next to me. It was March, so I knew football season was over. After a few minutes, the gentleman to my left asked, "Are you Leonard Slatkin?"

After confirming my identity, he proceeded to tell me about the many recordings of mine he had and his love of classical music. Curiosity got the better of me, and I inquired, "You came in with those other guys up here. What do you all do?"

"We are professional wrestlers."

He proceeded to introduce me to two of the others, and we spent the flight talking about Brahms, Shostakovich, and figure-four leg locks.

It is a good idea to make sure that the soloist is somewhere near the door that leads to the stage prior to a performance. I cannot begin to tell you how many times the orchestra tunes and then everybody sits around waiting for the pianist to make his or her entrance.

There are different reasons for the problem. Sometimes the artist can't hear the call to the stage over the paging system. Sometimes there is no paging system. A few soloists simply take their time on the journey from the dressing room.

The same goes for getting the public back into the hall after intermission. Many are still at the bar and want to finish their drinks before heading back in. A few would just as soon stay there rather than listen to the second half. Before signaling the concertmaster to tune, the stage manager should be told that the libation area is clear.

One of my favorite pastimes is looking for errors in the program book. Once, in Pittsburgh, we learned that Sibelius was born in 1684, and in Washington, the instrument list contained something called the "suspended piano."

Here is what I think should be included for every piece on a program:

- The birth, and if applicable, death dates of the composer
- The year the piece was written
- Who gave the world premiere and where it took place
- Whether the current performances are national or regional premieres
- The orchestra's first and most recent performances of the work
- A full instrumentation list
- How long the piece lasts—a helpful gauge for listeners

Some conductors enjoy speaking to the audience prior to leading a particularly difficult or new piece of music. If you are one of them, the key is to be brief and succinct.

Do not overanalyze, and never, ever talk down to the public.

If needed, have the orchestra demonstrate a passage or two to familiarize the audience with stylistic elements they will encounter. Sometimes injecting a little humor in the talk is helpful. If you are not comfortable improvising the talk, memorize the key points and make it appear as though you are speaking off the cuff.

And always, even with a microphone, make it seem as if you are talking to people in the back of the auditorium. Sometimes the lighting makes that difficult, but being inclusive can make all the difference in the world.

Lastly, it is okay to tell the audience how the piece ends. It is not a whodunit.

Always shake the concertmaster's hand before acknowledging the applause upon your entrance. The same goes at the end of each piece. If there is a soloist involved, he or she decides whether to share the applause with you. Sometimes soloists forget you are there. Don't let that bother you.

When you come offstage, let the soloist have the first bow alone. Sometimes guest artists will insist that you join them onstage. Follow their lead, but express how much the audience will love seeing them by themselves one time. If they keep at it, and if there is enough applause, encourage the guest artist to play an encore, but usually something between three and four minutes. This is not the time for the Liszt Sonata.

Be gracious at autograph signings. Several of my colleagues blow this off, but so many people bring programs and CDs. They spent good money on this, and you want them to come to your next appearance.

There is one man in the Tokyo area who comes to everything I do in Japan. He always brings at least six recordings. This has been going on for years. Sometimes he brings an issued version I have not seen before.

Do not be surprised if you are asked to sign a mobile phone cover, a ticket from the concert, or even a CD of a piece that you just played but that is performed on the disc by someone else. After a set of John Williams film-music concerts, I autographed more of John's recordings than mine—understandable, as I have not recorded any of his film music.

If you are given flowers at the end of a concert but are leaving the next day, my suggestion is to pass them on to one of the orchestra members onstage. It is a nice gesture, especially if there has been a lovely solo from a particular musician.

Gentlemen, if you are wearing a tuxedo or suit, button the jacket. I know it is more comfortable open, but it is distracting to the orchestra to see the front flapping around. Make sure you go to a tailor and have your jacket altered for your gestures so the back lies flat while you are conducting. There should also be plenty of room under the arms. It means pretending to lead the orchestra in the fitting room, but this will pay dividends in the long run.

Long ago I learned the hard way not to comment on anything regarding ladies' fashion choices. I remember a violinist in Tivoli who had a fairly large tattoo on her shoulder and back, highly visible to the audience. Not sure how to deal with that.

Anne-Sophie Mutter was among the first to play in strapless gowns. I believe it was the critic Martin Bernheimer who wrote something to the effect that "we should all be grateful that Isaac Stern keeps his shirt on."

PART THREE

———

THE BUSINESS
OF MUSIC

Music is spiritual. The music business is not.

—Claudio Monteverdi

THE AUDITION

A CAUTIONARY TALE

*If you have a job without any aggravations, you don't have
a job.*

—Malcolm Forbes

One

Susan had feared this moment for a very long time. After an
interminable period of waiting and warming up, she was summoned to the stage. A job hung in the balance, one that could
determine a path for the rest of her career.

The personnel manager brought her through the door and
announced, "Candidate Number 16." Onstage were a music
stand and a piano. A series of panels, about eight feet high, were
placed from one side of the proscenium to the other. Susan did
not know who was on the other side of the wall, nor how many
people would be listening.

She had been told not to speak and that any verbal communication had to go through the personnel manager to the
assembled crowd. For months Susan had been practicing the

required concerto and orchestral excerpts. She knew that she would start with a solo piece and that someone on the other side of the curtain might stop her, probably after three or four minutes. Taking a deep breath, Susan launched into the Mozart D Major Concerto.

A lone voice intoned, "Thank you. Let's move on to the excerpts." For this audition there were six pieces, in varied styles. The order had been determined earlier in the day and would be the same for each applicant. It had been made clear where she was to start and where she was to stop. There could be no deviating from the plan.

Everything seemed to go well, except for one short passage during which her grip on the bow momentarily relaxed. Susan realized that this might cost her the position, but she continued with the remaining pieces. Once again the words "thank you" were uttered, and she was escorted off the stage.

Such is the nature of an audition for an orchestral position. In a profession that relies on communication and flexibility, none is evident in the harsh ten minutes spent playing for one's life. Years of studying, practicing, and honing one's skills are reduced to this single defining moment.

It was not always this way.

Two

In the early days of orchestral life, the conductor controlled the audition process from beginning to end. There were no committees or juries to pass judgment. If the music director heard or saw something he—always a he—liked in a candidate, that person was hired. In some cases an actual audition might not have even taken place; the conductor simply brought in someone whom he favored. There was nothing the musicians or unions could do about it. Just try telling Toscanini, Reiner, or Szell whom they could and could not hire.

As musicians acquired more say in the selection process, different methods of choosing who would play in an orchestra emerged. Let's point to our example of the above violinist. How did Susan get to this point, and what was the process?

First, of course, there must be a vacancy in the orchestra. This can occur when a musician retires, leaves for another job, or is terminated, or if the group is looking to expand. An advertisement is placed in the American Federation of Musicians magazine, and the date of the audition is announced. Sometimes an orchestra will also send out the notice to music schools as well as other orchestras, in the hope that they can lure the cream of the crop.

If the vacancy is for one of the orchestra principals, such as concertmaster or first clarinet, feelers might go out via email, phone, or personal contact. Sometimes members of the orchestra themselves might try for advancement from within the group. For example, the fourth horn might be interested in moving up three chairs, as this is one of the plum jobs, offering more solo work and quite a bit more money.

Each professional orchestra has its own rules and regulations governing auditions. What follows is a general glimpse at the process, with many aspects taken from different ensembles.

Some groups are more restrictive and others more liberal, but the following version is fairly close to what is common among the majority.

Three

Susan had learned of the orchestra job opening from seeing a notice on the bulletin board at the conservatory, where she was in her second year of a master's program. She realized that no piece of paper or diploma would tell anyone of her talent. It was time for her to perform and audition and get into the job marketplace. She needed to earn a living.

Susan was taken to her first concert when she was six years old. It was an orchestral program and featured one of the most prominent violin soloists of the day. Enchantment struck, and she immediately asked her parents if she could take up the instrument. Lessons ensued. Progress was made, and the young girl dreamed of standing in front of a great orchestra one day and playing the Brahms Concerto.

Through eleven years of diligent study and constant practice, Susan had three different teachers, each one guiding, criticizing, and cajoling her to do better. At one point she was reduced to tears and considered quitting. But she knew that she had the gift and toughed it out.

There was no question of what Susan wanted to do after high school. Her application for one of the country's leading music schools was accepted, and she packed up and headed east. Her teachers were strong and dedicated. One of them had actually been a decent soloist but never quite made it to the big time. He told his young charge that although she was very talented, there really was no way she would become a world-famous soloist.

Although disappointed, Susan sought out others who were in a similar situation, and along with three other string players she formed a quartet. After all, chamber music seemed like the highest of the musical art forms, and this would certainly be a more than acceptable way of making a living.

But doing this while continuing her studies proved an impossible task. And as she delved further into the repertoire, it became clear that a professional string quartet would have great difficulty in a limited market for their product.

The bulletin board at school advertised about fifteen orchestras with vacancies in their violin sections. The level of these groups ranged from those that had fifty-two-week seasons and paid a minimum of $100,000 per year to some whose season was not even half that and projected about a $32,000 annual wage. There might be other opportunities in those communities as well, such as freelance work or teaching. So an acceptable yearly income was certainly possible.

Four

Susan decided to try for something in between. A city in the Midwest promised a forty-week season along with perks and incentives. It would be her first professional audition, and she did not know what to expect. After communicating with that orchestra's personnel manager, she received a packet with all the information.

The first round of the audition would not even be conducted in person. Each candidate was to submit an audio recording that included a concerto and a couple of orchestral excerpts. Susan learned that there would probably be 150 applicants for this one position. Although she had performed in public several times, she had no audio clips of her performances that would provide the required excerpts.

Now she had to hire a pianist, an engineer, and a studio to make the demo. This was unexpected and cost a bit more than was in her budget. In the end, the ten-minute CD was shipped off to the orchestra, along with a detailed curriculum vitae. There was one item on the questionnaire that was surprising. "Are you a member of the American Federation of Musicians?" Although union membership was not a requirement for the audition, it would be necessary to join if the position were offered.

Since she was an American citizen, there was no problem with Susan's legal status. But one of her colleagues was at school on a student visa. He had also thought about auditioning for the same orchestra. Again, it was possible to play for the committee, but he would have to be able to work out his residence status if offered the job.

The two of them passed this preliminary phase and were asked to come for the second round of the audition, which would be held in the city where the orchestra resided. Each applicant had to pay for plane fare and any accommodations they might need if they advanced to the third round. The two of them flew out together and wondered aloud what would happen should either of them win the job.

It was mid-February, and there had been a light snowfall that day. Worries that the flight might be canceled had sprung up in Susan's mind the day before. She was used to harsh conditions and took care not to slip on the ice as she came out of the motel the orchestra had booked for her.

Five

They both arrived at the hall at 8:00 in the morning on that snowy Saturday. There were thirty-five other violinists vying for the position, but the order of who would play when had not been determined. About half and hour later Susan was informed that she would perform around 11:45, with fifteen others coming before her. Her friend was not so lucky. He would audition sometime after lunch.

There were seven practice rooms available. Those who were not among the first to play waited in the orchestra lounge. As soon as one violinist went to the stage, another would take his or her place in a small warm-up room. This meant that Susan had to wait about an hour and a half before taking the violin out of its case. Of course she had gotten up quite early to practice some scales and arpeggios before getting in the taxi and heading to the hall.

The night before the audition, the members of the audition committee had played a demanding program with a guest conductor, and this evening there would be a repeat performance at a different venue, followed the next day by a Sunday matinee back in the hall. There was a hall rental by a couple of outstanding jazz artists that night, making it impossible for auditions to be held after 4:00 in the afternoon. Each contestant knew that if they advanced, the semifinals would not be held until Monday.

Susan wondered if her placement in the middle of the pack was a good thing or not. She certainly did not want to go first, as that position would most likely be the standard by which all the others were judged. But with a tough concert the night before, how tired would the committee be? And who actually was on this jury?

For the violin auditions, a group of eight members of the orchestra were self-chosen and paid for time served. The concertmaster and associate, as well as the other principals of the string section, were on the committee. Two more members of the violin section rounded it out. After spending three days sorting out the audition CDs and listening to a preliminary round of those who chose to audition live, the judges had whittled the number of contenders down to thirty-five.

As usual, they were not told anything about the candidates. Matters such as age, experience, gender, and nationality were simply not to be considered. That's because, forty years earlier, an applicant who felt that she was not selected for the orchestra because of her race had filed a lawsuit. Although the suit was dropped, the impact of even a hint of prejudice was enough to prompt the use of a screen during the audition process to guarantee anonymity.

Yet, the ethnic makeup of the orchestra was quite diverse even in the 1970s. And today women constitute close to half of the orchestral personnel. Musicians came from various backgrounds, and no one in the ensemble ever questioned the ability of those chosen through the audition system. None was given preferential treatment, but at that time, without the presence of a screen or carpeting to shield the sound of high heels, and considering the fact that the committee had full résumés of the contestants, it was possible that someone with vast experience could have a leg up. The issue of favoritism also might rear its head.

The orchestra members gathered in the auditorium fifteen minutes before the scheduled start of the audition. They were told that two of the thirty-five candidates did not arrive, so the field had been narrowed. Each member of the committee had a notepad to keep tabs on how the candidates did, and each had his or her own way of keeping score. Some simply assigned a plus or minus; others made more detailed notes.

At this point in the proceedings the music director was not involved. He would join the committee only for the finals, which would be held on Monday afternoon. That is the norm for most auditions. In this case, he was still in Japan, with a concert that night. Everyone settled into their seats, mostly scattered away from each other, staring at the partition that separated them from the violinists.

Six

The sound of the stage door opening signaled the beginning of a long day. The concerti were all by Mozart, which, after the Beethoven, probably are the most difficult for making a positive impression on other string players. Susan had wondered why she would even have to play a concerto at all. The likelihood of her performing anything like that with the orchestra was virtually nil.

Most of the candidates fell far short of what the musicians were looking for. Intonation was spotty at best. Some had no concept of how to play a proper staccato, and others chose unusual tempi for the orchestral excerpts.

Susan got to the warm-up room after sitting around for more than an hour. The only person she knew was her friend from school; none of the others was from her conservatory. Some were very young, and there were clearly some violinists who had been members of orchestras in other parts of the country. She struck up a conversation with Howard, who appeared to be in his mid-forties.

"Is this your first time auditioning?" he asked.

"Yes," Susan said. "I'm a bit nervous."

"Well, the best I can offer is just go out there and imagine that you are playing for yourself. It will be strange with the screen up and trying to figure out what the jury looks like."

Susan wanted to know about this man.

"I play in an orchestra about forty miles from here. My family loves the area, but with kids now getting ready for college, I need to make more money. This is the third time I've tried for a position here. So far, no luck."

"Did you think you played well the other two times?" Susan asked.

"On my first try I was intimidated by the screen. My current orchestra isn't really big enough to have followed the same rules when I auditioned years ago. I just stood in front of the conductor and concertmaster and they picked me. It was all quite comfortable. The second time here I felt I did better, and I really do not know why I was not selected. I have been told that the person they picked was the most technically accomplished of the applicants, but I know her. She has no soul. Maybe these days all you need are the chops."

"What will you do this time?"

Howard replied, "I have practiced my butt off and feel good about the excerpts. The problem is that damn Mozart D Major. My strengths are really in the Romantic and twentieth-century repertoire. I wish I could play Tchaikovsky instead."

Seven

Susan felt pretty good about her Mozart, as she had performed it with the student orchestra two years before. Yet, many of the orchestral excerpts were not pieces she knew well. Susan downloaded a couple of files and heard varying interpretations. One of the pieces was the first movement of Prokofiev's Classical Symphony. The two versions she listened to were wildly different, and she had no idea which tempo the committee was looking for.

At 11:55 a.m. Susan was summoned to the stage. The assistant personnel manager led her to the door. It was time to begin. The Mozart was good and the excerpts seemed fine, except for that little mishap with the bow. The music stand had started to slip down, which momentarily threw her, causing just a little jiggle in her bow arm. Her recovery was fast, but no one on the other side of the screen could have known what occurred. To them, it was a hiccup in Susan's audition.

When it was over, Susan packed up her fiddle and returned to the waiting room, hoping that the committee had chosen her to advance to the semifinals. Everyone needed a break for lunch, and sandwiches were brought in for both contestants and jury. Since neither side was supposed to see each other, the orchestra members ate in the auditorium while the applicants hung out in the lounge.

After an hour, the auditions resumed. Susan's friend played second after the break and seemed pleased with how he had performed. Howard was not so happy.

"I totally screwed up the Mozart! There is no way they are going to pick me. Maybe it's time to consider an orchestra farther away from home."

The musicians, having listened to all thirty-three aspirants, cast a secret ballot to determine who would move forward. There was no discussion, and each member was allowed to pick as many or as few as they wished. The personnel manager and his assistant tallied up the information and announced that seven violinists had received more than half the votes. These violinists would play again on Monday.

Susan was getting nervous. No one was talking very much, and there was a palpable tension in the air. Finally the personnel manager came in and named the lucky seven who would move on. He thanked everyone else for his or her participation. If there were any questions about continued accommodations for the remaining contestants or what would happen on Monday, his assistant would be glad to answer them.

Both Susan and her pal were selected. As he had predicted, Harold was sent packing. There was disappointment from some, while others were resigned to the decision, and those selected were relieved. The two friends decided to go out for dinner, but each knew that they would be competing against one another in thirty-six hours.

Eight

Monday began quietly at Symphony Hall. The sound of a lone vacuum cleaner could be heard as Susan entered through the stage door. A table was set up once again, with members of the staff greeting the violinists. This time, as there were just the seven contestants, each had his or her own warm-up room. With auditions slated to begin at 10:00 a.m., coffee and donuts were provided. Susan did not eat but managed to drink a glass of orange juice.

The members of the committee started arriving and headed straight for the auditorium. Since this was the semifinal, the music director was still not involved. He would arrive around noon and wait for the announcement of how many contestants had advanced to the final round. The repertoire was pretty much identical to that in the previous round, but some of the excerpts had changed. Once again the screen was up and the carpet was down.

Each violinist was told the order of when he or she would appear. Susan was third. Now that she was used to the surroundings, she felt much more comfortable and played with more confidence. Not prone to nervous outbreaks, she finished the ten minutes and left satisfied.

Her friend was worried. There was something not quite right with his instrument; he had noticed it during his morning warm-up. It was possibly a misaligned sound post inside the violin, but there was nothing he could do about it. There was no string technician on hand, and there would be no way to explain to anyone that this might be the cause of a slightly diminished sound from his fiddle.

The committee joked around a little before the first competitor walked through the door. Once auditions were under way, all sat in diligent silence, each keeping notes. The process took less than two hours, and after a secret ballot, it was announced that only two of the seven had garnered more than half the votes. The musicians agreed that this would be the total number who would advance to the finals.

By this time all the candidates had gathered in the orchestra lounge. The atmosphere was surprisingly relaxed, considering that so much was on the line. The violinists did not speak much about how they played; instead, everyone simply bantered about their lives, telling stories of how they had become instrumentalists in the first place.

Without warning, the personnel manager appeared and gave out the news. Susan had advanced, along with a much more seasoned veteran. Her friend did not make the cut. Susan tried to console him, but his head had already left the room and the rest of him now followed, to get a taxi for what would be a very long trip home.

There would be an hour lunch break, with the final round commencing at 1:00 p.m., at which time the music director would join the jury. The conductor was in his room, awaiting word. It had been a grueling couple of weeks on the road, and he was tired and jet-lagged. The news that there were only two finalists made him feel slightly better. He used the next hour to do a little studying for the coming week's program. It was all standard repertoire, but some brush-up was in order. The hour passed quickly.

He had not seen his orchestra for a while and greeted the committee in a friendly manner upon entering the auditorium. Once again the personnel manager outlined the rules of the finals for the jury and the conductor.

"Each contestant will play part of a concerto of their choosing. You can stop them whenever you would like. After that, they will perform a movement of a solo Bach piece. There will be ten excerpts, but if you want to hear more, just let us know."

The jury settled into their comfy seats and looked ahead at the screen, which remained in place. The conductor hated it. In this most personal of professions, why would one select a musician in the most impersonal of ways? Still, this was the way of the world, and there was nothing he could do about it.

Susan, now identified as Candidate No. 1, was up first. Her concerto of choice was the Brahms. Although certainly difficult, it began in a way that showed off one of her strengths: a big sound. She made it all the way through to the tutti prior to the development. She was glad that she did not have to play the cadenza; she worried that it might tire her out for the remainder of the audition.

The prelude of the E Major Bach Partita followed. Perhaps this was too obvious a choice, but again she felt good about how she interpreted the work. Some of the excerpts were the same as in the previous rounds, though a couple of them were new. All of the repertoire had been known in advance, and there was no sight-reading, although the application form said there might be. Susan thought she did well overall.

The music director sat by himself, listening intently but once in a while thinking about a passage he had looked at during the lunch hour. As Candidate No. 1 played, the maestro was impressed by what he heard—the dynamic range and the technical command of the instrument. However, it became fairly clear that in the excerpts, this violinist was pretty new to the orchestral world. It was something that might influence his thinking.

Candidate No. 2 arrived onstage. He was more seasoned than Susan, and it showed in his handling of the excerpts—not a slip or misjudged tempo anywhere. The solo pieces were less satisfactory, but the audition was for a section job, not a solo appearance. He finished up *Don Juan*, and the conductor was heard saying, "thank you," just as he had done at the end of Susan's performance.

With the stage now clear, the deliberations began. The music director was asked to go back to his room while the committee discussed, voted, and made its recommendation. After almost twenty minutes, the conductor was informed that the vote resulted in a tie, four to four. Neither violinist had a majority, and this meant one of two things: Either no one would be selected, or the two had to return again and play once more.

The music director thought about it and decided that another round was in order, but this time it would be without the screen and would be referred to as a superfinal. This was possible because the actual finals had adhered to the rules. There was a little objection on the part of two of the committee members, who said that anonymity was still important, but the conductor argued that he wanted to be able to voice comments directly to the candidates and receive feedback if needed.

Susan was quite surprised to learn that she would be playing again. Having given her all, she was not so sure that yet a third appearance that day would work in her favor. The two contenders were told that all the committee wanted to hear were three different excerpts, no concerti. A coin was flipped and Susan won, opting to start.

It seemed strange to finally see the jury. Another plus: the actual size of the auditorium was now clear to her.

With the screen down, the identities of the two violinists were revealed. The conductor and orchestra members could now determine from the contenders' applications where they had studied, where they had played before, where they lived. The concertmaster went up on the stage and asked Susan to play the dreaded Classical Symphony excerpt first. He gave the tempo from his seat near the center of the auditorium.

It was slower than Susan had prepared, but she managed to play it cleanly. Next up was the first few bars of the Brahms First Symphony. When she finished the conductor asked her to do it again but to use the full bow this time. Lastly, she played the scherzo from Schumann's Second Symphony. All three pieces were standard fare at almost any audition, and everyone knew the tricky spots. Susan dashed it off and could see nods of approval from the jury members.

She had done her best. Now all she could do was wait.

Obviously our story does not end here, but the audition process, per se, does. Anyone who has ever undergone this, either as a participant or jury member, knows how grueling it is. But here is the important question: is it fair?

On the surface it would appear that the answer is yes. Identities are kept secret. It is impossible to determine the race, gender, or physical appearance of the entrant. Votes are done by secret ballot. What could be wrong here?

Let me cite examples of how this process actually works against the best interests of an orchestra. Some groups hire a number of substitutes and extra musicians to play in the orchestra on a regular basis. They are clearly fine performers and excellent citizens. Some participate in the orchestra's educational and chamber music programs and play at fund-raisers. A few have been playing for several full seasons with their respective orchestras. What they do not have are the benefits given to the fully contracted musicians.

There is only one thing they do not do well: audition. Who knows why? It might be their nerves or a lack of confidence when playing alone, and perhaps it is simply not in their nature to deal with this kind of stress. Is it really right to ignore fine musicianship, proven in the workplace, just because a player might have had a rough ten minutes behind a screen?

Shouldn't there be some way to allow experienced musicians some leeway? What may have been routine for them when they first auditioned many years ago is now difficult, as the nature of the audition process has moved (in a way similar to solo competitions) toward an attitude of technical excellence above all else.

And what about the screen itself? Standing like some sort of Berlin Wall, it does the one thing that is not supposed to exist in music: place a barrier between the performer and the listener.

These days symphony orchestras are for the most part exemplars of nondiscrimination. There was a time when few women were hired, but now that this has changed, isn't it time to give our auditioning committees the opportunity to make decisions without the impediment of a screen?

There are many who insist on more racial diversity in the nation's orchestras, but how is this to be achieved behind a screen?

Several musicians I have spoken with said that they do not believe they would have won the job if they had not been hidden.

The obvious rejoinder is, "How do you really know that?" There are no guarantees of either success or failure. Ultimately, the decision is a judgment call. Even with a screen in place all of the time, there can be compromising circumstances that verge on discrimination. For example, in Detroit we had a flute audition at which the only two musicians to make it into the finals were two existing members of the section. Certainly the majority of the committee knew the characteristics of those players. How could this audition have not been prejudiced in one way or another? We identify musicians by how they sound, not how they look.

Can these dilemmas be solved? Here are some possible solutions, based purely on my own experiences.

Both the personnel manager's office and two musicians from the orchestra, usually from the section where the vacancy is occurring, could review the applications. If there were candidates with at least two years of experience playing with an orchestra, they would be immediately advanced to the semifinals. All others would either submit a CD or appear in person if the first round was done live.

The second round, as well as the first, would be done behind the screen, as there would be no need for communication between the jury and competitor at this point. The screen itself would be placed near the musician-judges rather than immediately in front of the candidates. It is impossible to know how the barrier affects the sound quality, even though it would apply equally to all performers. Still, if it is placed nearer to the audience, there is a better chance of hearing the true acoustic properties of each individual in more natural surroundings.

With the screen up and close to the candidates, there is no way for them to know what kind of space they are playing into. This is a critical, physical part of the process. The science of acoustics demands that we know the parameters of sound. It affects how we project our personalities. With the screen moved into the hall itself, the candidates would know the true dimensions of the space and be able to project their sound accordingly without the intimidating presence of the screen at such close proximity.

The screen should be removed for the semifinals. By this time the jury should be allowed to know who is auditioning, with all the résumés in front of them. Direct contact should be possible, allowing the contestants the opportunity to interact with the committee. The overall atmosphere should be welcoming and cordial, not impersonal.

At the finals the same conditions should apply. It is in this round that the candidates might also be asked to play some ensemble passages with current members of the orchestra. The conductor might actually go onstage and lead a few excerpts, learning whether or not the contestant can follow and adjust.

Today's orchestras play a much more varied repertoire than those of past generations. However, it is rare for an audition to acknowledge that pops, film music, and jazz are performed with great frequency during a season. Often these are presented after one rehearsal, or possibly two. It is my feeling that the sight-reading part of an audition should include an excerpt in one or more of these styles in order to gauge the candidates' versatility.

These simple changes to the audition procedure, at least as it stands for most major orchestras in the first quarter of the twenty-first century, could make all the difference in the world for everyone. Such adjustments would bring greater dignity to the process and at the same time keep integrity intact. The process must remain fair to the candidates while also ensuring that the orchestra is well served. Rewarding excellence based on a combination of talent, experience, and emotion is certainly a positive.

Epilogue

Susan paced anxiously while her friend took his turn onstage. When he returned, his face was ashen.

"How is it possible that I practiced the wrong Schumann symphony?"

He flung his music into a corner, sat down, and sobbed. Inside, Susan was exuberant. It was not her nature to be self-satisfied, but this time she knew the job was hers.

Indeed, a few minutes later, the personnel manager came to the room to tell her that she would be offered a contract. He led Susan back into the hall where the members of the jury and conductor applauded and congratulated her. It turned out that three musicians knew her, and she already was starting to feel at home. The job would start in September, but since the position was already vacant, she could start at any time.

Susan thought about it and decided to finish her degree, just in case. After working out the details, she was given a copy of the Collective Bargaining Agreement—the contract between the musicians' union and management. It was explained that she would have a year and a half of trial in the orchestra, with three tenure reviews along the way.

The next chapter of her life was beginning.

STOP THE MUSIC

You are never strong enough that you don't need help.

—Cesar Chavez

Three hundred and sixty-five days make a year, but for some music lovers, 2013 seemed like an eternity. That was the only conclusion that many could draw after what may well have been the ugliest labor dispute in the history of American orchestras. Fifteen months after it started, almost nothing of positive value came out of a situation that no one predicted.

That it would occur in Minneapolis came as a great shock to almost everyone in the music industry. After all, this was a city where progress was partially measured by how well the arts were doing. The opera seemed to be flourishing, the Guthrie remained one of the country's theater jewels, and the Minnesota Orchestra was basking in outstanding reviews and a Grammy nomination.

So what turned a seemingly healthy organization into the dysfunctional family it now appeared to be?

Before we begin, it is important to understand that although this historic meltdown took place a few years ago, it continues to represent the struggles that most American orchestras are going through. Following the equally debilitating strike in Detroit in 2010–11, I found it interesting to follow and analyze this situation as an objective observer to more fully understand the nature of labor negotiations in the twenty-first century.

Let's turn back the clock a little. The storied history of the Minneapolis Symphony includes tenures of such noted maestri as Dimitri Mitropoulos, Ormandy, Antal Doráti, Stanisław Skrowaczewski, and Sir Neville Marriner. After much debate the orchestra underwent a name change in an effort to attract more attention from the state legislature. With the St. Paul Chamber Orchestra across the river, a spirit of friendly competition existed, but some wondered if two orchestras were too many for the area.

My own relationship with Minnesota began in the early 1970s, when I was asked to create something new for the summer season. Orchestra Hall, a gleaming structure in the heart of the city, was a perfect venue for adventure, with a large plaza outside and many spaces inside. And after a few experimental seasons of concerts with the seats covered by a large platform and the audience sitting on pillows, we arrived at the ideal solution— Sommerfest.

I served as the founder of that festival as well as the orchestra's principal guest conductor, and those years were some of the happiest of my musical life. I loved the orchestra, the public, the board, and the management. Sommerfest incorporated concerts indoors, outdoors, and all around the town. The plaza was turned into a vibrant marketplace and became a gathering point for the good citizens who lived and worked downtown. It was a utopia.

As my career took me in different directions, so too did the Minnesota Orchestra change in several ways. There were four different music directors during my time with the MSO, a new concert hall was erected, and the summer was now bursting with orchestral and chamber music. But despite changes in musical as well as community leadership, all seemed just fine in the Twin Cities. The orchestra had a very secure contract, and there were boasts of balanced budgets. There was absolutely no reason to suspect that anything was wrong.

While most orchestras made their constituents aware of hardships due to the economic storm of 2008, including my own in Detroit, Minnesota seemed unsurprisingly quiet. It was always taken for granted that the arts scene in the Twin Cities would be unfazed by economic upheaval. The stoic Nordic temperament most certainly would not be affected by the rumblings that now distracted other ensembles around the country.

By 2012, however, we were starting to hear that all was not well in the land of lutefisk. Discontent was emanating from blogs and chats. Still, with a contract deadline approaching, somehow we thought that everything would be resolved.

Then, wham!

A new contract proposal from management contained many more drastic changes than anyone could have predicted. The first offer included a 30 percent wage reduction for the musicians. There were also more than two hundred work-rule changes suggested by management, which led to the musicians feeling abused. No one believed the numbers that were being tossed about. The orchestra refused to even vote on the offer, and as the season approached, management declared it had no choice but to lock out the musicians.

A lockout occurs when the board will not allow the musicians to return to work under any conditions. A strike occurs when the musicians do not accept the terms of the board. Ultimately, the result is the same: no music, no pay, and no benefits.

It did not help that the musicians' colleagues across the river in St. Paul were up the same creek without a paddle—and now the area was without both of its professional orchestras.

The board was accused of mismanaging the funds to make ends meet, but to my knowledge the musicians never questioned where the money was coming from. This would be the first of many errors. It seems that when things appear to be going well, no one checks up on reality.

Vicious posts went up daily from the musicians, railing against anyone who did not support them. The executive director was accused of every ill, with vitriolic fervor being par for the course. For the most part the board remained silent. Day in and day out board members read that they were miserly; in effect, the musicians were biting the hand that fed them.

It is traditionally not the place of a music director to get involved in the labor process. Most of us are not in a union, and we generally elect to remain neutral as employees of the board and leaders of the orchestra. But Music Director Osmo Vänskä spoke out nonetheless, ever so gingerly, in support of his musicians and then, less than subtly, by threatening to resign. Given

imminent concerts scheduled at Carnegie Hall, Vänskä may
have thought his threatened resignation would cause all parties
to come together quickly. But that was ultimately not the
case, and to add insult to injury, at least one person interpreted
Vänskä's intentions to be self-serving:

> Many of us truly miss the Orchestra. Yet I am bothered that
> the deadline that might get it done has nothing to do with
> bringing classical music to a Minnesota audience. It is all
> about a concert in New York City. This speaks volumes for
> the values of Vänskä, management, and the board. Serving a
> local audience clearly doesn't matter. Getting a good review
> in the *New York Times* is the only priority.
>
> scwebster
> August 29, 2013
> 9:37 a.m.
> *Minneapolis Star Tribune*

This came on top of an announcement that the Swedish record
label BIS had decided not to record an upcoming album by the
orchestra:

> BIS officials say they are withdrawing from the September
> sessions because they no longer believe the orchestra is "in
> good-enough shape" to meet the exacting standards the
> label requires, according to a document obtained by MPR
> News.
>
> August 19, 2013

What struck many as strange was that the label thought the orchestra would not be ready to perform, but Carnegie Hall apparently did.

Besides financial barriers, threats to cancel Carnegie Hall concerts and future recordings, and an increasing air of hostility, there was another negative effect of the labor war: many musicians auditioned for and won positions with other orchestras.

Depending on which side you listened to, the number of musicians who vacated their positions varied wildly. The orchestra's website featured a photo of the full ensemble with the members who had left whited out. This was misleading, since the whiteouts included retirees and vacancies that existed before the lockout. By one count, the number of musicians lost reached twenty-seven. However, the Minnesota Orchestral Association (MOA) listed half a dozen as having actually left as a result of the stalemate.

Those Carnegie concerts just might have to be played with almost one-third of the membership filled by substitutes or extras. This would send a dangerous message, one that the musicians' union was certainly hoping never to see: that you can field a great orchestra without all the regular members of the institution. And should the notices be negative, all the posturing about the importance of these performances would be for nothing.

A mediator was brought in, no less a figure than the former senator George Mitchell, who had successfully brokered a peace agreement in Northern Ireland. Could this world-renowned figure accomplish the same result in another dispute? The musicians roundly rejected his first suggestion, and the board dismissed his second.

With a new deadline approaching, one that could signal the departure of the music director and the postponement of any kind of season announcement, another proposal was put forward by management. It was applauded by the blogosphere supporters of the musicians but on closer examination did not appear to be much different from a previous offer. Essentially, the orchestra was being asked by Senator Mitchell and the board to return to work at their old salaries for two months, enough to ensure that the season would commence and the first of the Carnegie trips could be preserved. During that time negotiations would continue, and if no accord was reached, reduced salaries would come into play for the next two years.

Riding in to put in their two cents' worth was a group of one hundred composers.

> We know—with certainty—that the cancellation of the Minnesota Orchestra Composer Institute will have a lasting and negative impact on American music, and we urge you to act now to resolve the lockout and reinstate this essential training ground for the cultivation of talented composers.
>
> August 15, 2013
> WQXR blog

One could not argue with the sentiment, but as with most issues, it all came down to money. The MOA had put substantial funds toward this project, and the composers did not suggest how that money could be raised in the current economic climate.

At this point you might be wondering why I was so intrigued by a situation that was not about my own orchestra. The answer is simple. Even though each institution has its own set of problems that must be solved in an individual way, we all must work to preserve what is left of our orchestral landscape. My interest in the dispute was not so much about salaries or rankings, but rather about great music not being made available to the orchestra's constituents. The Twin Cities were being deprived of performances by their two ensembles, despite ad hoc presentations during the lockouts. Ironically, some of the conductors invited to participate were those who had received negative evaluations by the players prior to the lockout.

Management and board made themselves scarce. The executive director was accused of all manner of improprieties, in particular of taking raises and bonuses before and during the lockout. The board chair and others, who had backgrounds in the banking world, were viewed with skepticism amid allegations that they colluded to destroy the orchestra. The usual calls for resignations appeared, but there were no alternatives offered as to who might take their places.

Members of the Minnesota board, orchestra, and management came to Detroit to find out how things were managed during the DSO strike. One of the things they discovered was that an organization called "Save Our Symphony (SOS)" had been formed privately to create audience awareness via the internet.

Interestingly, in an effort to make it more difficult for a similar organization in Minneapolis to organize via the web, the MOA bought up web domain names that might have been useful to an organization like the SOS. This was discovered by an intrepid blogger who made it out to be a conspiracy worthy of the Kennedy assassination:

> This looks like deliberate, predatory domain buying meant to outwit and irritate angry patrons and donors.
>
> This looks like the MOA colluding even more intensely with Detroit than we've been led to believe.
>
> This looks like the destruction was premeditated and pre-ordained from the beginning. From BEFORE the beginning.
>
> This looks like the MOA didn't just want to pick a fight with musicians.
>
> This looks like the MOA wanted to pick a fight with their patrons.
>
> [insert your rage here]
>
> Well. You know what, MOA? If you thought the following scenario was ever going to play out, you're even more fricking delusional than I thought . . . and as you know, I think you're pretty fricking delusional already.
>
> Emily Hogstad
> Song of the Lark
> August 21, 2013

As the deadline for an agreement approached the ten-day mark, the MOA released its third financial report, paid for by the board and without projections into the future. The news was bleak, and for the first time management acknowledged that the music director, the Carnegie Hall performances, and indeed the next season were all in danger. It was becoming very clear that an old saying was true: "When someone says it's not about the money, it's always about the money."

The DSO came back into the picture when the Detroit-based group SOS tried to convince the Minnesota board that recruiting new musicians would not be easy. The SOS misstated the number of musician vacancies in Detroit and tried to make a case that the DSO was not attracting viable candidates at auditions. This undermined the good work that the SOS had done over the previous two years and certainly did not help its relationship with the new musicians or board. It was also blatantly untrue.

At some point, one had to wonder how the union played into all this. Naturally, one of the accusations was that management was trying to bust the labor movement. With right-to-work laws now being enforced in more and more states, there was certainly some credibility to this argument. Here is what the union writes about the benefits of becoming a member:

> The AFM negotiates wages and working conditions in order to maintain minimum standards for its members involved in recording, TV shows, music videos, commercials, films, video games and traveling theatrical productions.
>
> Afm.org

I don't see anything mentioned regarding symphony orchestras.

Negotiation is done by musician representatives whom each orchestra hires and pays. The union pretty much stands on the sidelines, waiting to see how the eventual solution will impact other groups. The top-tier orchestras are rated almost solely on the size of their budgets and the pay scales generated by the contract, hence the focus on being a top 10 ensemble.

The Minnesota Orchestra only entered this elite group of ten after other orchestras, such as Philadelphia and Detroit, starting making drastic salary cuts. It has always troubled me that outstanding orchestras are rated simply because of pay. Are St. Louis, Dallas, and Cincinnati, among others, really inferior in musical ability and accomplishment? Certainly not. And just because an orchestra drops to the number 11 position, should it be considered inferior? The appellation "regional" was often attached to any orchestra not in the top 10 group. Of course, there was never a definition of "regional," much less a rationale for why that would be a negative.

Something else that should be considered in any negotiation is cost of living. The most highly paid musicians are, of course, those who can put more money in the bank after expenses are paid. The wages of a Cleveland Orchestra member would not go so far in New York or San Francisco.

A big issue that has come up recently concerns how much an orchestra actually works in a given week. After all, to the average person, it is difficult to understand a contract in which only twenty hours of work in a week are accounted for. Musicians argue that much of their work takes place away from the stage, through individual practice, study, and instrument maintenance.

But the truth is that this varies wildly from player to player. Some may only take out their violin for the work periods contractually intended, and for a few that is enough to produce an outstanding result. Others work prodigiously making reeds, fine-tuning passages, and working with colleagues. While musicians approach their preparation in various ways, the standard orchestra contract provides a common base salary, beyond which individual players can negotiate for additional pay.

The settlement in Detroit brought some degree of innovation as the next contract approached. The board chair and musicians were determined to settle a new agreement six months prior to the expiration of the old one. With a ten-year plan in place to put the orchestra on stable financial ground, a framework for honesty and openness appeared. In what marked a major shift in my own thinking, I volunteered to help broker various artistic concerns that might come up.

A few years before the expiration of the Minnesota contract, the board authorized $52 million to refurbish the half-century-old Orchestra Hall. Most of the money was to go into a redo of the lobby area, with a little left over to deal with deteriorating elements in the performing space. No one questioned this allocation of funds at the time, but almost immediately after the lockout it became a divisive issue between board and orchestra. A separate renovation fund had been set up well before any negotiations began, and it was made clear that any donations going to this project could not be utilized for any other purpose. When it was discovered that existing money was being taken out of the endowment to help cover some of the construction expenses, many questions arose regarding how deeply in debt the orchestra might really be.

How could management and the board raise this money for the hall but at the same time find it impossible to support the musicians? Of course construction had begun and could not be halted, meaning that the revenue was already committed. This issue would persist throughout the tussle. The battle cry was, "What if they built a hall and there was no one available to play?"

As the lockout's one-year mark loomed, an event was held to celebrate the renovated but musicless Orchestra Hall. Patrons and donors gathered, at $750 per person, to check out the enhancements. From atop the second floor they could see the musicians and their supporters out in the plaza area, demonstrating for their cause. The days were creeping by, and deadlines were moved back. Journalists were getting tired of the story as well. The musicians of the orchestra announced more concerts they would present on their own. Mediated sessions resumed, and new proposals were generated. The gala reopening of the hall took place without participation by the musicians of the Minnesota Orchestra.

The governor of Minnesota and the mayor of Minneapolis announced that they would be making a statement to the public. Could this be the long-awaited news of a settlement? No. In fact, there were thunderstorms in the area, and the news conference had to be postponed. Perfect irony. And when the two leaders finally appeared, the totality of what they had to say was, "The two sides need to sit down together and work this out." Square one? Or zero?

In a very strange and not well thought out move, some musicians and supporters floated the idea that the orchestra and Osmo should go to Carnegie on their own! Leaving aside the financial implications, they were now putting themselves in exactly the position they fought against for a year: fielding an orchestra with many substitutes and extras and passing it off as the real Minnesota Orchestra. In the unlikely event that this would actually occur, would the board allow use of the institution's name?

The board tried again, bypassing the mediator to make a fourth offer. They proposed reducing instead of increasing salaries over a period of three years to achieve a maximum $6 million in debt—ironically, something the board had earlier said would be impossible to sustain. Since this proposal was made just three days before the dreaded September 30 deadline, it appeared to represent a final offer. Another problem with this offer was that it was presented to the press, once again violating an agreement by both parties to keep everything private.

The orchestra members rejected the offer, this time with just forty-eight hours to go before the deadline. But of course that date had changed several times during the lockout. All that kept resonating was that the Carnegie Hall appearances were in jeopardy and that the music director might leave. Fate also had it that on the same day this offer was rejected, news reports said New York's City Opera would declare bankruptcy, and the United States government might shut down owing to collapsing negotiations in Congress.

One year almost to the day after the lockout commenced, a last-ditch proposal was presented by the members of the orchestra. Its rejection led to the cancellation of the Carnegie Hall concerts. Vänskä had told a Finnish newspaper that he would resign at midnight if the orchestra was not back rehearsing within the week. True to his word, the announcement went up the next morning. The orchestra seemed in shock, as if they could not believe it had actually happened. Sometimes people make good on their threats.

What can be learned from all this heartache?

Here are my ten suggested starting points for all parties involved in a labor negotiation:

1. No matter how much each side may believe the other is the enemy, there are always those who have compassion and understanding for the opposition. Well before any talks commence, determine who best represents your point of view but has respect for what the other side thinks and believes.

2. Financial information must be made available from day 1—not only how much money the organization has, as well as its investments, but also the true salary that each musician earns. An independent auditor needs to be brought in to oversee these documents. Transparency equals trust.

3. The board must come up with a projection of how far it is prepared to go with its deficit. The orchestra must understand that organizations cannot operate in the red as they used to. Instead of small losses, orchestras are now seeing debts moving into the millions of dollars. And

with more board chairs seeing the effect of large deficits in corporate America, they have begun to impose the same standards on nonprofit organizations.

4. At least two members of the orchestra should be on the board, thereby allowing open discussions that would then be taken back to the musicians. However, the same rules for membership on the board must apply to the musicians as well. There is a minimum dollar amount that each board member must pay to serve. The membership of the orchestra could pool their resources to make their voice equal to that of any other member of the board.

5. Obsolete work rules should be updated and rule changes presented not only to the negotiating committee, but also to the whole membership.

6. There must not be comparisons made to any other orchestra's base salary or situation. Every negotiation is local. No more top 10 nonsense.

7. Start taking cost of living into account. This has been a no-no for such a long time that many have lost sight of the fact that a decent wage means different things in different places.

8. All parties must agree not to leak information. The bloggers can't be stopped, but they only muddy the waters. It is vital that during negotiations everyone involved agrees to say nothing to the press or public. It only leads to speculation and does nothing to aid in finding proper solutions to serious problems.

9. If, after a few months, negotiations stall, change the participants on both sides. It's what they do in hockey during a face-off, and it can work here. Fresh faces mean new ideas.

10. Most important, remember who is losing: not only the orchestra, not only the board, not only the management, but also the public. These are the people who have supported everyone with donations and ticket sales. They are the backbone of the business, and we must treat them with the utmost respect.

One final item. If you are a music director, stay out of it unless both sides ask you for advice. Even then, mostly listen. You can lay out some artistic goals you would like to achieve, but address only those that are meaningful for the contract. And never, ever say anything to the press.

On January 14, 2014, the lockout ended. With musicians facing the loss of unemployment benefits and the board looking at a possible revocation of the license for Orchestra Hall, each side finally reached the endgame.

But for almost a year and a half Minneapolis was without its resident orchestra. Everyone tried to put a good face on the settlement; however, it was not difficult to read between the lines. Without a music director, with so much bitterness, and without really knowing what public support was left, it was clear that a very long road to recovery lay ahead.

Less than twenty-four hours after the Minnesota compromise, the Detroit Symphony Orchestra announced that it had reached a new three-year deal with its musicians. This occurred eight months prior to the expiration of the old contract. One orchestra continued to rise from the ashes. The other would have to climb much higher to get above the debris.

Minnesota's road to recovery was given a strong boost when the music director decided to revoke his resignation. More and more, the orchestra and board realized that their responsibility to the community came first.

Relations between the board and the orchestra have improved immensely. The Minnesota Orchestra has made successful trips to Europe, Carnegie Hall, and Cuba. It used to be that when things went well, it was because the orchestra played great, and that when they went badly, it was marketing's fault. Not now. The players have become more friendly to the audience and will even bend contract rules in the interest of selling tickets.

Money remains a difficult issue, as it is with almost every major American orchestra. How every orchestra handles future negotiations will be under intense scrutiny. It is a rough road the vast majority of arts organizations must travel these days.

I'LL PUFF...

You have to have really wide reading habits and pay attention to the news and just everything that's going on in the world: you need to. If you get this right, then the writing is a piece of cake.

—Terry Pratchett

O ver the years I have had the opportunity to put various thoughts into print, and I wished to include a few of them in this volume. Some introduce a concert or series. Others arc satirical. There are miniature "think pieces" about certain elements within the music industry.

When I was in high school, music and writing were the only things that really interested me, apart from baseball. A few short stories, mostly science fiction, were submitted to various publications and, rightly, rejected.

I tried to emulate some of my favorite writers, including O. Henry, Roald Dahl, Ray Bradbury, and Saki. But these were just pale imitations; I had no feel for original content or style. When my professional life bloomed, I put away the typewriter. Writing by hand was also off the table, as my orthography can be deciphered only by a pharmacist.

Gradually, as different musical projects emerged, I was asked to write a few words, sometimes for a program book, other times a newspaper. Imagine the thrill of seeing my byline in the *New York Times* and London's *Guardian*! It was wonderful to see a youthful dream fulfilled.

Here are a few of the articles.

"Fanfare for an Uncommon Man"

The Guardian
October 27, 2000

Aaron Copland, who was born one hundred years ago, was the greatest of all American composers. Leonard Slatkin explains why he will never grow tired of conducting his music.

He is the American West. He is the heartbeat of New York. He is the musical voice of a nation. And he would have been one hundred years old this year. Aaron Copland, who died in 1990, is more than just a figure of American musical history. He stands as a pioneer in a country of innovators. When we think of the composers who have made their impact on the world scene, only a few names from America come to mind: Charles Ives, George Gershwin, Samuel Barber, Leonard Bernstein, and at the top of the list, Copland.

Why at the top? Why not? Who else saw us through the musical turmoil that was the twentieth century? Certainly it can be argued that Ives (1874–1954) was the first to give a truly national flavor to the music of America. But his was an isolated vision, followed by few at the time and misunderstood by most. Gershwin gave the nation a sense of popular identity, but his few works for the concert hall showed an imitative gift that was not allowed to develop in his all-too-brief life (he died at the age of 39).

Samuel Barber (1910–81) reinvented the romantic from the past century, but he rarely strayed from his literary path. Bernstein should have inherited Copland's mantle, but will probably be remembered more for his performing abilities rather than his creative output, with the exception of *West Side Story*, his one astonishing Broadway flourish.

If I am being unduly harsh on these masters, it is hardly out of lack of respect. They were all giants, and it is impossible to envision the American musical landscape without their vital contributions. But Copland has them all beat by a mile.

In this centenary season of his birth, many are wondering if it is necessary to have any celebrations at all. It is not as if his music is not heard often in the concert halls of the world. The ballets—*Billy the Kid*, *Rodeo*, and *Appalachian Spring*—are familiar to concertgoers. His Third Symphony has a place in America similar to Walton's First Symphony in Britain. Pianists of all nationalities perform the Piano Variations. The music for the 1949 movie *The Red Pony* stands alone, like the film scores of Prokofiev and John Williams. He created the only clarinet concerto in the twentieth century that is actively in the repertoire of all clarinet soloists.

Copland could roll comfortably with the times, whether creating works of overt nationalism such as *Lincoln Portrait*, his 1942 work for speaker and orchestra, or throwing himself into serialism, as in *Connotations* (1962). At the rehearsals for the premiere of the latter work, Bernstein remarked that no matter what the idiom, "you always sound like Copland." And maybe that is the key. He always had a recognizable voice. Or rather, voices.

Copland spent his student years in the early 1920s in Paris, studying with the great French composition teacher Nadia Boulanger. It was she who encouraged him to find individuality in his compositions. His response was the Symphony for Organ and Orchestra. At its premiere, conductor Walter Damrosch said: "If a man of twenty-five can write music like this, in five years he'll be ready to commit murder."

In listening to his early works, it is hard to find much that could be criticized so harshly. Yes, there is an edge to the music, but hardly anything that wasn't being done by most of the composers of the time. Could it have been the first hints of the use of popular rhythms that put Damrosch and others off? Possibly, but what so many failed to hear was the original message Copland was bringing. Those open sonorities that would carry him through so many pieces can clearly be detected in the first major works.

When I was a student at the Juilliard School in New York, one of the test pieces for entrance into the college was *El Salón México* (1937). Copland was intrigued by the music of his southern neighbors. He went on to write the *Danzón Cubano* and *Three Latin*

American Sketches. But *El Salón* would be the work that gained him real attention in the concert hall.

It remains a challenging piece, with complex meter changes and shifting speeds. All of us in the conducting class were terrified of it, very much as we were of Stravinsky's *The Rite of Spring*. The trouble was that none of us saw the fun that Copland was having. If we had not concentrated solely on the technical demands and gone for the intent, I suspect the metric obstacles would have been much easier to surmount.

Perhaps the work that sums up the man and his music is the Third Symphony (1946). This is a product of the Second World War, and it is meant to uplift and mentally strengthen those who play it as well as those who listen to it. This piece brings together most of the compositional styles that Copland had been employing for almost twenty-five years. The open sonorities of the introduction remind us of the ballets. The raucous scherzo sounds like those murderous intimations of his early pieces. The slow movement is lyrical but at the same time harmonically harsh, calling to mind some of the passages in the solo piano music.

Then there is the finale. Beginning with a reworking of his *Fanfare for the Common Man*, we take a contrapuntal journey into jazz, folk, and blues idioms. At the climax of all this, a strident chord disrupts the flow of the work. It is like a colossal scream of agony, similar in intent to the opening of the last movement of the Beethoven Ninth or the cry of the orchestra in Mahler's Tenth. Ultimately, all conflict will be resolved. The fanfare will combine with the main tune of the first movement. The ending is pure celebration and optimism.

It is not possible to get tired of conducting Copland. There is always a challenge, be it the simplicity of *Quiet City* (1941) or the jaggedness of *Inscape*, which forms part of the program for the BBC Symphony Orchestra's *An American Portrait: Aaron Copland*. You must be clear to the orchestra at all times, but you must also know when to stay out of their way. Much of his music seems to play itself, but that is because most of it follows logical musical progression. Copland always seems to know what note comes next. This sense of inevitability is a gift granted to only a few. He always knows when it is time to stop.

I met Copland only a few times. But the first has special meaning. In 1970 Copland came to conduct the St. Louis Symphony. I was just a twenty-five-year-old assistant conductor. It was my job to observe the rehearsals, help with balances, and make any relevant suggestions to the visiting conductors. What could I possibly say to the man who personified music in the U.S.? Not much, as it turned out. He knew exactly what he wanted, whether it was in his own *Music for a Great City* or Roussel's Third Symphony.

We had two performances in St. Louis and then got on a plane to play a one-off date in Iowa. I sat next to him on the flight, and it was really the first opportunity to talk. He spoke of the younger generation of composers, eager to learn from them. When it came to his own music he was quite humble. He did not play favorites with his works. They were his children, each with a character and personality of its own. He was enjoying his newfound career as a conductor and felt he had pretty much written himself out.

As we descended, I asked him to autograph one of his scores for me. I whipped out my battered copy of the *Appalachian Spring Suite*. On the inside title page, he wrote, "To Leonard, from his friend Aaron Copland, in the air, March 1970." I have only one other signature on a score and it is from Benjamin Britten. He simply signed his name on the *War Requiem*.

Two complicated and simple men, not so different and yet separated not just by continents, but by whole worlds of musical thought. And yet they both have that voice. The one that tells you who they are in every single bar of their music.

It is one hundred years. And Copland is still with us. With all of his voices very much intact.

"Bridging the Musical Gap"

The Washington Post
June 21, 2003

Remember when you went to a concert with your kids? No, not 'N Sync or Britney Spears. And not just dropping them off and waiting to pick them up. I mean actually sitting in the hall and listening to a symphony together.

Ever wondered how a composer's life affected the way he or she wrote the music? Or if social and political events of the time changed the way music sounded? Or even how long a composer lived and how that person died?

You now have a chance to answer some of these questions and, in the process, perhaps discover that classical music is important and that we must ensure its survival. The National Symphony Orchestra is launching the first of its "Composer Portraits" next weekend. These are concerts designed for families and anyone else interested in learning more about those who created the masterpieces of the symphonic canon.

Much has been written about the decline of music education in our schools over the past thirty years or so. I was a product of public education through twelfth grade in the California school system. By the time I reached my final year of high school, we had three choruses, two bands, an orchestra and a composer-in-residence (who happened to be Peter Schickele). It is doubtful that such a rich cultural education for our young people is taking place these days.

I used to think that most of our problems in the professional arena regarding audiences and shrinking funding were the direct result of a lack of arts education. And I still think that is a problem. But recently I have begun to suspect that there is more at work.

About two months ago I was in Los Angeles, doing some television work on a documentary about Hollywood and the composers from Europe who settled there. Because L.A. was the place of my childhood, we decided to incorporate into the documentary what it was like to grow up there during that era. One of the places we used as a location was the house where I was raised. My parents worked as musicians in the film studios and continued to work as classical instrumentalists as well. The guests who came through our home read like a who's who of the music industry: Igor Stravinsky, Frank Sinatra, Arnold Schoenberg, Art Tatum, Nat King Cole, Erich Korngold.

The parents of the current owner were there to greet the crew and me. They knew who I was and knew something of the history of the house. A few minutes before we wrapped up, their daughter, the current owner, appeared. To my surprise, she had no idea of the musical talent that had crossed the threshold of her home. But more shocking was that she did not know who Stravinsky, Schoenberg or some of the other luminaries were. In other words, the parents did not transfer their knowledge and love of music to their offspring. A huge musical gap seems to exist between generations.

The "Composer Portraits" are a small step in bridging that gap. Adults and youngsters will have an opportunity to share a unique musical experience. The first part of the concert will be a musical biography of Tchaikovsky, this year's featured composer. Martin Goldsmith has written, and will read, a narrative that will follow the composer through his life. At certain points, we will play the music accompanying this time frame. Social matters and political climates will be addressed so we can understand the period and circumstances during which the works were created.

The second part of the program will feature one work: Tchaikovsky's Fourth Symphony. But, before we perform the work, we will spend about ten minutes playing excerpts and showing how they fit into the overall scheme of the piece. In this way, members of the audience will have musical guideposts that they will be able to recognize as the complete work is played.

After the performance, everyone is invited to stay and participate in a discussion of what they have seen and heard.

I hope that over the course of the next several seasons we will build a collection of these portraits. They could then be offered to other orchestras. Schools could use them as an educational tool. Families would have a way of enjoying a concert together.

Most of all, I hope that these portraits will bring all of us closer to understanding the lasting value of great music and art.

"MUSIC; Inauthentic Beethoven, but Authentically So"

New York Times
February 15, 2004

In the guest conductor's dressing room at Avery Fisher Hall, three items adorn the walls. One is a part for the flute from Dvořák's "New World" Symphony. The other two are pages from the scores of *La mer* by Debussy, and Beethoven's Symphony No. 7. All three bear liberal markings and alterations from two conductors who led those works with the New York Philharmonic: Gustav Mahler and Arturo Toscanini. Visitors are reminded that not only were both gentlemen music directors of that august institution, but they also altered what composers had written, a practice much in vogue for most of the last century.

Throughout music history, from the time the standard repertory developed, performers have added their own personal touches to past masterpieces. This comes under the heading "interpretation." The conductor most identified with the practice of altering printed scores was Leopold Stokowski. But you have only to trace the performance history of Beethoven's symphonies to find all sorts of subtle as well as drastic changes. Conductors like Richard Wagner, Richard Strauss, Wilhelm Furtwängler, George Szell and Leonard Bernstein, to name a few, have all contributed to the re-orchestration of many works by old masters.

In Mahler's case, it is particularly important to understand the dual nature of his musical life. More respected during his day as a conductor than as a composer, he was one of the few who actually advanced the musical art on both fronts. It is his work as a composer that most people know now, but it is clear from the pages on the wall that his creativity was not limited to his own works.

Mahler prepared editions of the symphonies of Beethoven, Schubert and Schumann. The term he used was "Retuschen," "retouchings," more or less. Mahler never intended for his editions to be thought of as in any way his own compositions, but these changes did not go unnoticed.

"Erroneous" and "barbaric," screamed the *Neue Freie Presse* in Vienna. The *Wiener Abendpost* reported: "Each note is lighted up, the darkest pathways are illuminated, nothing is lost; the voices that murmur in the shadows are exposed to the glare of the sun, airy lines are weighed down, every nervous fiber of the melody is detached and isolated from the sound fabric as if with a scalpel."

The *New York Times* remarked after a performance of the Ninth Symphony: "He uses for some passages two pairs of kettledrums, which make a noise that passes beyond the bounds of musical effect. Elsewhere he accentuates the stroke of the drums with nerve-racking results, as in the scherzo, especially at the very beginning, where the rhythm is marked as by the shots of a rifle."

These kinds of alterations came in for renewed attacks as the early-music aesthetic of "authentic" performance took hold in the 1970s and '80s. But the editions are authentic artifacts of Mahler's era, if not Beethoven's, and valuable indications of what Mahler's performances must have sounded like.

On a tour that begins in Charlotte, N.C., on Wednesday and ends at Carnegie Hall on Feb. 27 and 28, the National Symphony will perform Beethoven's "Eroica" and Ninth Symphonies in editions prepared by Mahler. For listeners who have come to expect "historically informed" performances, these versions will come as a shock.

So what did Mahler really do, and why?

For a concert in 1900, he wrote, "Owing to an ear complaint that ultimately left him totally deaf, Beethoven lost his indispensable and intimate contact with reality and the world of physical sound." In addition, Mahler cited the changes that were occurring in his day in instruments and in the size of the orchestra.

He used the expansion of the orchestra to supplement and clarify many textures. In Beethoven's time, the string section might have had as few as six or eight first violins and perhaps a single double bass. Mahler could have twenty or more first violins and certainly would have competed with Strauss in using ten to twelve basses. Such a body of players would have drowned out several passages in the woodwinds. So Mahler frequently "doubled" instruments or added others to make sure that a particular figuration was heard. In the "Eroica" Symphony, for example, to a line that Beethoven had assigned to a solo flute, Mahler added a second flute and an E-flat clarinet.

Then there are the changes in the instruments themselves. The French horns in Beethoven's orchestral works would have been "natural" instruments. Lacking valves, they could not perform chromatic passages. Mahler, like many before and after him, simply filled in places where notes were missing. The range of most of the woodwind instruments had increased, too, so Mahler used the added notes to keep the flutes, say, from having to drop an octave for a note or two.

Beethoven used blocks of dynamic levels in his orchestral writing. So if a passage is marked fortissimo, the whole orchestra sees the indication. Conductors commonly adjust levels in these places. After all, the trumpets and timpani playing at full force can often drown out an important melodic line in the strings. Mahler is scrupulous in this matter. He makes sure that all of Beethoven's lines are heard clearly.

It is less clear how Mahler interpreted the pieces himself. Reports vary wildly, and we know that he was a spontaneous musician. Yet there are places in the scores where one can recreate Mahler's conducting style. At the start of the finale of the "Eroica," for example, Mahler notes that the pizzicatos represent a child trying to take its first steps and stumbling. To achieve this effect, Mahler added a slight accelerando, as if to exaggerate the child's attempts. The portamentos and Luftpausen (slides and silences) indicated in the parts will come as a shock to many.

It is also illuminating to see what Mahler does not change. No melodic lines or harmonies are altered. In the Ninth, the choral parts remain unchanged, but there are unusual breathing indications for the soloists. Most surprising, Mahler does not comment on the one thing that has caused the most controversy over the years, Beethoven's metronome markings, indicating the speeds of individual movements. Mahler himself abandoned metronome markings after completing his Second Symphony, so he may simply not have considered them important. Indications like "allegro" and "adagio" were enough.

Today we have moved toward a musical ethic that considers the printed text sacred. But most composers would have welcomed the advances in the development of instruments. Mahler realized that for his own music to survive, it would have to undergo interpretation by others. Great art flourishes precisely because it can be construed in different ways by succeeding generations. Seeing those pages on the wall with the markings of Toscanini and Mahler, we are reminded that music is a constantly evolving creative process. Hearing how those pages sound, no matter what alterations have been made, reminds us of the durability of those masterpieces.

"To Clap or Not to Clap"

Adaptistration
October 6, 2006

Concert season has opened around the world. Orchestras are tuning up, bringing out their musical gifts to the concert-going public. Most of the time, they know their efforts will be rewarded with rounds of applause. They just don't know when this will occur.

I was reminded of the difficult choice the audience must make in this regard, with a few concerts that I conducted over the past few weeks. In London, I was privileged to work with the outstanding pianist Lang Lang. He played the first concerto by Frédéric Chopin. The opening movement is a typical bravura statement from the heart of the romantic era. Although there is no formal cadenza (a portion of the piece where the soloist is on his or her own for quite some time), there are numerous passages that do not include the orchestra.

When we concluded the movement, several thousand people in the Albert Hall burst out with fervent, appreciative applause. Lang Lang acknowledged them with a bow.

A few weeks later, I was involved in a performance of the Brahms Violin Concerto with Gil Shaham. This was part of the National Symphony's opening subscription concerts, and the program was repeated three times. The Brahms does have an extended cadenza in the first movement. Very showy, and played brilliantly. On the first night, the audience applauded after the movement, but, surprisingly perhaps, the subsequent two audiences refrained from any kind of outburst other than coughing.

A few nights later we were performing the Tchaikovsky Violin Concerto with Joshua Bell. Once again bravura work with a cadenza full of pyrotechnics. Not only did the audience cheer vociferously after the movement, they actually awarded it a standing ovation. We still had two movements to go.

I cite these examples because it is clear that audiences do not understand the etiquette that goes along with their participation as part of the performance. "Should I or shouldn't I?" Most of the time, listeners just wait to see what others will do and follow suit.

But what do the performers expect?

Well, the argument against premature applause is usually that it interrupts the flow of the entire work. History tells us that this is a false assumption. At the premiere of Beethoven's Seventh Symphony, the slow movement had to be played twice due to the ovation it received in isolation from the rest of the piece. It was common for the audience to express its appreciation and demand, if not a repeat of a movement, at least an encore of another selection.

Most of the time, this dilemma is found in concertos. But there are a couple of orchestral works that have pitfalls as well. Perhaps the most famous occurs in the Tchaikovsky Sixth Symphony. The third movement of this work is an explosive march. If this were the finale, audience reaction would be thunderous. More often than not the audience cannot contain its enthusiasm and breaks into an audible reaction. Even now, there are many new listeners who are not aware there is an aching last movement to come, one of the great death scenes in all of music.

What is the real force that makes us want to applaud at moments when it would appear that we should not? It is simple. The applause is not only to acknowledge the performers and a particular portion of the work, but it is also a suitable way to break the tension and acknowledge publicly an appreciation of the performance.

What happens when no one applauds? The audience coughs and finds other ways to release the buildup of sitting for up to twenty-five minutes in silence. I remember a performance of Tchaikovsky's First Piano Concerto with Byron Janis that we did in Madrid. When the first movement ended, about four or five people started to clap, and 2000 others shushed them. Then they coughed and talked. It was five minutes before we could begin the next movement.

It is even worse in the opera house. When Tosca finishes "Vissi d'arte," shouts of *Brava!* rain down from the rafters. An ovation can continue for minutes. What happened to the dramatic flow of the text, not to mention an awkward musical transition that is lost? We don't applaud during a soliloquy at a play, and the aria is certainly the equivalent. Again, I believe we want to reward a fine performance and relieve the tension we experience in the audience.

How do the performers feel about it? I can only think of a couple that prefer the silence. And this is mostly the etiquette of the recital, which is a more intimate setting. We are delighted that the audience is enjoying the performance and wants us to know it. It also gives us time to catch our breath and readjust our mental and emotional attitude for what is to come next. Yes, it is inappropriate to applaud in the middle of a piece, and that does happen sometimes. But no sin has occurred. And there should be no embarrassment.

Once in a while something will happen that actually is inappropriate. There is a famous spot in Tchaikovsky's Fifth Symphony (him again). The music is loud and comes to a halt even though there are still about three minutes of music remaining. Unless one is actually trained as a musician, or already knows the piece, this place can be construed as an ending. Audiences around the world start to applaud here. On one occasion, the conductor actually had the orchestra stand up; he took a bow, went off stage, returned and brought his arms down to play the coda of the Symphony. Cute, but insulting to the audience.

In summation, it is just fine to express yourself at a concert. If you are moved by the performance or work, feel free to show the performers. That goes for not only cheering and applause, but the opposite as well. With the complaints we sometimes get about new music, it is now very rare for the audience to lustily boo. I miss that. How are we to know which music to bring back if we do not hear from the listeners?

So clap away. Just be sincere in your appreciation. Those of us on the stage will know that you really mean it and we will be thrilled. Just don't overdo it with lengthy outbursts that last well into the night. We all need to get to the restaurants before they close.

"Dischord at the Symphony"

Classical Source
May 1, 2008

"The average noise level in the orchestra during the piece was 97.4 decibels—a violation of new European noise-at-work limit." . . . So ran a headline in the *New York Times* on 20 April 2008 . . . and Leonard Slatkin's imagination is fired . . .

It was to be a very ordinary evening at Symphony Hall until chaos erupted quite unexpectedly. By the time it was over, two men had been arrested with another possibly being exhumed.

The case in question involved the rarely noticed Second Trombonist of the Upper Lakes Region Symphonia. The first half of the program had gone without incident. A Rossini overture followed by a Mozart piano concerto. It was only after the intermission that things became perilous.

An oversized orchestra was employed to perform Gustav Mahler's Symphony No. 1. It started out peacefully enough. The sounds of nature emanated from the instruments with birds chirping and other tame beasts under control. Then, about ten minutes into the first movement, all hell broke loose.

You sensed that something was up when the bassoonists, who sit near the trombone section, began to put their fingers in their ears. The visual aspect of this might not have been so disturbing, but the presence of Plexiglas panels all over the stage should have given us fair notice. In one shattering moment, the atmosphere of the concert hall was totally disrupted.

A uniformed policeman came running on, halting the performance. Rushing into the trombone section, he demanded: "Who has been making all this racket?" The bassoon section pointed fingers behind toward the culprit, James Sackbutt, currently the number-two trombonist in the orchestra.

The officer went directly to the offending musician: "You are in direct violation of the European Union Sound Act of 2008. The volume level you achieved was three decibels over the amount specified in Section 4, Paragraph 3 of the Code. You are hereby ordered to cease playing immediately."

"But the music specifically says fortissimo," argued Sackbutt. "Plus, the trumpets have a triple-forte at the same time, and I don't see you giving them a citation."

"I can only track one player at a time. And they simply did not appear on the sonic radar gun."

Sackbutt countered: "Besides that, the conductor asked me to play the passage loudly. He is my boss, and I am not supposed to argue with him."

Officer William Guardate then moved to center stage to confront Maestro Massimo Extremo. "Did you knowingly encourage Mr. Sackbutt to play above the decibel level prescribed by the European Sound Union?" "No," replied Extremo. "I was simply trying to obey the instructions left by the composer some 120 years ago. No one complained about it then, and I do not see why we should be complaining about it now." "The law is the law," said Guardate. "I must insist that you and Mr. Sackbutt accompany me to the police station, where charges will be filed."

Twenty minutes later, a district judge ordered that the composer be contacted about his role in the matter. "But he has been dead almost one hundred years!" responded a frustrated Sackbutt. "Surely you cannot find out what he intended regarding volume levels. And there were no regulations about volume back then."

Judge Camilla Jurisprude then issued a court order for the exhumation of the body of Gustav Mahler, in the hope that some DNA evidence might be uncovered which could exonerate the two musicians. "It could be that something in Mr. Mahler's genetic code caused him to over-achieve when it came to issuing instructions to the musicians."

In the meantime, the orchestra has been ordered to play nothing other than music by Grieg and Delius for the remainder of the season.

"Change Is in the Air"

Classical Source
September 27, 2009

[This one actually got me in trouble, as several people thought it was for real. I intended it to appear as if it were a press release by the DSO, but clearly more than a few readers were appalled.]

A reflection by Leonard Slatkin, kick-started by the hostile reception that greeted the first night of Luc Bondy's production of Tosca *for the Metropolitan Opera, New York*

> *Harsh booing at the gala opening night of the Metropolitan Opera—where strong negative reactions are rarely heard, at least in comparison with European opera houses—was still ringing in the ears of the opera world on Tuesday.*

—*New York Times*, September 23, 2009

The Detroit Symphony (of which Leonard Slatkin is Music Director) has announced plans for a completely revamped season, starting with its concerts this week. The programs will not be changed, at least the ones advertised, but the manner in which the works are performed will be altered.

To begin, the orchestra will be seated with their backs to the audience. Music Director Leonard Slatkin said at a press conference yesterday, "I feel that the listeners are distracted by seeing the faces of the musicians. With the players turned around, I believe people will tire of looking at backsides and focus purely on the music."

But that is only the beginning of the new era. For the final work on the program, Rachmaninoff's Second Symphony, the conductor is not only going to reinstate the cuts sanctioned by the composer, but will add some additional ones as well. All in all, the total performing time will be about twelve minutes.

"The piece is so long and repetitive. Once you have heard the main tunes, well, they are so memorable that they do not have to be played again."

Slatkin went on to say, "It is my hope to perform a Bruckner cycle using this philosophy. In that way, we can get through all of them in one concert, perhaps with time for the two that have no number as well."

Beethoven's Fifth will get a trimming, but with a different rationale.

"Many years ago, I did a production of *Tosca* in Hamburg. The director told me that since everyone knows the opera, he wanted to eliminate many of the traditions that have bogged the work down. So there was no church in the first act. The heroine did not leap to her death at the end. Yes, we were roundly booed, but I started wondering whether the same rationale could be applied to symphonic music."

So for these performances of the overly familiar Beethoven score, the opening five bars will not be played, since everyone knows how they go. It will be straight into the sixth measure. In fact, every time the four-note motto comes in and is played loudly, the passage will either disappear or be performed softly.

Most of the soloists will be surprised to learn that the tuttis that usually herald the first entrance will go away. So no more three-minute intro for either the Brahms First Piano Concerto or Violin Concerto.

Slatkin has a reason for this as well.

"We are not paying them to sit or stand around."

Other emendations include orchestration changes. The opening of Stravinsky's *The Rite of Spring*, played by the bassoon in a high register, will now be intoned on the tuba, two octaves lower than printed.

"Tubists at the beginning of the twentieth century were not as facile as today's artists. Bassoonists have plenty of solos. Why not let someone else have a chance at it?"

There will also be a chamber version of Mahler's Eighth Symphony, sometimes referred to as the "Symphony of a Thousand." Slatkin hopes to get it down to forty-six musicians, chorus and soloists included.

"There are fine chamber versions of the Fourth Symphony and *Das Lied von der Erde*, so precedent is on our side."

Another of Slatkin's projects is to present the complete organ works of César Franck, transcribed for accordion. These will be played at the orchestra's pre-concert recitals.

Then there is the "Pictures Project," a round-the-clock set of performances including the thirty-three known orchestrations of the Mussorgsky classic. Long an advocate of alternate versions of the Ravel, Slatkin said, "It is impractical to include one on each of our subscription concerts. So we will start on a Friday, and keep playing until we get through all of them. If we lose a member of the orchestra along the way, so be it."

Finally, in keeping with the new seating arrangement, the orchestra will perform in street clothes, but the audience is requested to come in formal attire.

"Let them learn how long it takes to put on white tie and tails."

Season tickets, subscription renewals and cancellations can be taken care of directly with the DSO box office.

THE ROCK AND
THE HARD
PLACE

When people don't want to come, nothing will stop them.

—Sol Hurok

For as long as I can remember, going to a concert has always been an exhilarating experience. You never know what is going to happen. Perhaps the performance will be sublime. Or maybe it will disappoint. There is a sense of anticipation from most in the audience, even though some are attending out of a sense of duty and some, having been dragged along, are hoping to catch some shuteye. Nevertheless, when the lights dim and the door opens, the start of a concert signals the beginning of an adventure.

So what are we to make of all the remarks, both spoken and written, regarding how our audiences don't seem to care? They are not showing up. They are getting older. Classical music is no longer relevant. The performers are simply going through the paces. The stagehands are paid too much. Why do we need orchestras in the first place?

There are no easy answers to any of these criticisms. The so-called fine arts have always been for a relatively small segment of the population. Perhaps that is why the term "elitism" is thrown around so liberally. I searched for a few definitions of the word. Many were vague, but one from Dictionary.com caught my attention: "representing the most choice or select; best."

Think about it. Isn't this what most people should be striving toward? Remember the slogan, "Be the best that you can be"? Why is that commercial phrase any different than "Be elite"? But this is just a simplification of what is clearly a larger problem affecting virtually all aspects of the artistic world.

It is a subject that most of us in the performing arts have been trying to deal with for quite a long time. As previously mentioned, when I began my career as assistant conductor in St. Louis, one of my first assignments was to lead the world-premiere concert performances of *Jesus Christ Superstar*. This work started life as a recording project, well before its stage incarnation, and took off to break all kinds of sales records. It spawned newfound religious zeal among some. The "rock opera," as it was referred to, was not really an opera or rock music in the true sense of the words as they were used in the late 1960s.

But there was no question that a marketing bonanza was at hand. We played two shows, and both sold out within a couple of hours. Clearly the audience was different from that traditionally seen at Powell Hall. Back then no one really paid much attention to demographics, and it was difficult to tell whether or not the orchestra had actually made new friends who would convert to fans of Sibelius or Bruckner at some point.

In 2012, in Detroit, we put on a show with the singer-song-writer Kid Rock. This came about because after a six-month work stoppage, it was critical to raise some big bucks fast. Two local entrepreneurs, Dan Gilbert and Matt Cullen, put it together. I contacted Rob Mathes to do the arrangements, and the show was presented at the five-thousand-seat Fox Theatre. It raised more than $1 million and sold out in record time. It also gave me the opportunity to say to the orchestra, without fear of reprisal, "Okay, let's move on to the next song, 'You Never Met a Motherfucker like Me.'"

Again, as at the St. Louis event, there were thousands of new faces, some mingling with longtime DSO subscribers. Barriers were shattered. But more than that, the concert helped put the orchestra in front of a whole new group of listeners. It did not matter if they returned. Not everyone in the city enjoys baseball, yet they all know who Miguel Cabrera is—the Detroit Tigers' star first baseman. Now people who had never heard of the Detroit Symphony were at least made aware of its existence.

But these events, and virtually all the others of similar ilk, are only onetime shots. They do not address any of the problems outlined at the beginning of this chapter. As the twenty-first century rolls along, more and more arts institutions are trying to do things in a nontraditional way.

In 2014 the New York Philharmonic began a two-week series called the Biennial, based loosely on the Viennese concept, an event held every two years to showcase new art. The presentation highlighted more than fifty works by composers from across the world. The Philharmonic, however, did not perform on most of the programs; rather, smaller New York–based ensembles played the Biennial concerts. And at that, most of the venues had limited seating.

For me, leaving aside the artistic decision to isolate contemporary music, I wondered how much it all cost. Music had to be rented or commissioned. Even those Philharmonic musicians who did not participate as performers had to be paid, and so did the outside groups. What was the pricing structure for the tickets? Assuming that some of the events were underwritten, how many people actually purchased those tickets?

And most important, what did it produce in the end?

I wasn't there and could only judge by the various reports in print and online. Everyone seemed to agree that it was a worthwhile venture, but no one spoke about the bottom line. And each was looking forward to the next such event. But again, where was the money coming from? Given that the Philharmonic, like so many arts institutions, had been struggling with fiscal shortfalls, was this really a true indicator of where orchestras should be heading?

My answer is yes—if we limit the number of weeks for these types of projects and they generate new audiences. Just look at the adventurous Carnegie Hall project, Spring for Music. For four years, orchestras that would not normally have gotten to Fifty-seventh Street played unusual and diverse programs for New Yorkers and people from their hometown audiences. Carnegie paid some of the expenses, but the orchestras had to make their own way and cover hotel, per diem, and the like.

When I took the DSO there, we played two programs, including the four symphonies of Charles Ives performed in one night. The Ives performance brought instant glory to the orchestra, as the majority of the press and public loved it. Other ensembles, some of which were making first New York appearances, also did well. These were amazing weeks of music.

But reality kicked in. It simply cost too much for everyone, and the project died after four years. It would be resurrected, with a somewhat different focus, three years later in Washington, D.C.

The flip side of the Biennial coin could be seen a few weeks after the contemporary music project. For the past eleven years the Philharmonic has presented a series called Summertime Classics. These programs fall somewhere between the standard fare presented during the season and what the Boston Pops used to do during the time of Arthur Fiedler: in other words, pieces that are familiar, if not played so often these days.

So it came as a bit of a surprise to read this commentary by Zachary Woolfe in the *New York Times* on July 3, 2014:

> Perhaps Wednesday was just a letdown after the orchestra's forward-thinking June programs. Last month began with the NY Phil Biennial, a kaleidoscopic, largely rewarding survey of new and recent music, and continued with a cycle of Beethoven piano concertos over which brand-new works by Anthony Cheung and Sean Shepherd had been dolloped like maraschino cherries. None of it felt stuffier than Wednesday's Summertime Classics installment.

Hey, the series is called Summertime Classics. What did he expect, a Stockhausen retrospective? Look at any summer festival by a major orchestra in the United States. Where are the bleeding chunks of contemporary repertoire? Only at the Tanglewood Music Center can a major symphonic ensemble showcase a full week of new music. And these new works are not played by the Boston Symphony but rather by an orchestra comprising highly gifted students who have been selected as fellows. There are other festivals devoted to new music, but none has a higher profile than Tanglewood.

Summer is the time for a break from the world of new repertoire for orchestras. Many of them have to play two or three programs a week, with several programs getting just one rehearsal. There is simply no time to practice properly and learn something new. As it is, there are always additions to the personnel of an orchestra who are seeing standard repertoire for the first time.

Once, at the Hollywood Bowl, I planned a program called "What the Bowl Taught Me," a poor pun on a popular song by Dvořák. It included works such as Georges Enesco's Romanian Rhapsody No. 1, the Overture to *Zampa* by Ferdinand Hérold, and an orchestral version of the Liszt Hungarian Rhapsody No. 2. When I was a boy attending Bowl concerts, these were staples of almost every season.

Looking at the fresh faces of the Los Angeles Philharmonic musicians, I realized to my horror that few of them had played or even heard most of this music. There was only one rehearsal, and we barely got through the concert. I decided that I would never again plan a program like this on such limited practice time.

But returning to the situation of the New York Philharmonic's Biennial and Summertime Classics series, once again I found myself puzzled. The questions that troubled me remained unanswered. What was the attendance? How much did the program cost to put on? Was it underwritten? How much were the tickets?

This brings me to the main point of the chapter: the relationship between creative vision and fiscal responsibility. Certainly artists would love it if we never heard the word "budget" ever again. But all over the world orchestras are suffering from various forms of economic woes. And many of them are criticized for a lack of variety in programming.

There must be some form of artistic vision that can be coupled with fiscal responsibility. Is it possible to have it both ways? If nothing else, the economic downturn of 2008 taught us that institutions simply cannot spend what they do not have.

There is a statistic that is thrown around and is mostly accurate, at least for the United States: A bit less than one-third of an orchestra's budget comes from the actual ticket sales. The rest is due to the largesse of its patrons and contributors. After the big fiscal meltdown, a substantial portion of contributions dried up. Some companies and individuals lost up to 80 percent of their portfolios. Clearly the motivation for donating to the arts was now seriously diminished, since the tax breaks and incentives amounted to almost nothing.

It is no surprise that contributions and ticket sales decreased sharply. A few institutions had the foresight to start new trends before the economic chaos set in. Orchestras in San Francisco and Los Angeles, for example, had already forged some paths in new directions many years earlier. At first they were met with adulation from the press but little enthusiasm from the public. As the seasons progressed, both sides were won over, and in some ways the adventurous wound up being what both orchestras became known for, sometimes overshadowing their contributions to what is generally called the "standard repertoire."

When James Levine was music director of the Boston Symphony, he brought back some of the Serge Koussevitzky tradition by introducing his audiences to new, but in this case quite thorny, music. Although Levine's bold move was lauded by critics, the trouble was that the public was not buying it, and for the first time in quite a while getting tickets for BSO concerts was, on occasion, not a problem.

The Cleveland Orchestra had a unique way of combating economic travails at home. Although their audiences had been relatively steady, contributions were less plentiful. They began a series of residencies outside of their hometown, namely in Miami, Vienna, and Lucerne. At first there was a great commotion in Cleveland: many felt that the orchestra was abandoning its hometown priority. But at the same time the organization was generating revenue and finding creative ways to entice local corporate sponsors to use the orchestra as an avenue for developing business partnerships abroad. As collaborations with funders evolved, the organization returned to some initiatives at home that kept the Cleveland Orchestra as part of the city's mainstream culture. It was still a risk, as the long-term viability of such a venture was unclear, but at the time it was seen as a forward-thinking concept.

Let me spend some time here telling you what we tried to do in Detroit to balance the need for artistic expression with fiscal responsibility.

At the conclusion of the musicians' strike in April 2011, what most people were not told was that during the conflict the major players in the dispute had been meeting privately. These sessions were not about solving the difficulties but were rather focused on what to do once a contract settlement was reached. I was fully involved in this process, seeing small groups and individuals, including members of the orchestra, in order to formulate plans for the future.

After six months, the strike ended, and one day later several initiatives were under way, all of which had already been discussed among leadership on both sides.

Clearly some sort of concert calendar had to be announced. Getting artists at the last minute was not easy, so we wrote off previous plans for the remainder of the season in favor of simply bringing the orchestra back onstage and the public back into the hall. Free concerts were played for the remaining two months, with contributions accepted from those in attendance.

During that summer multiple new programs were put in place, and each has continued to make an impact on both the artistic and fiscal sides of things. With a new chairman of the board coming on, there was certainly opportunity for change. But how could we get a disgruntled and resentful orchestra involved? What reasons did the board itself have for investing in the future of the orchestra?

Let's begin with the idea of reaching a different audience, something the musicians of the orchestra actually started on their own during the strike by giving several concerts in the suburbs. We decided to follow this example, playing to our usual audience as well as reaching out to first-time concert-goers, hoping that many would eventually take the opportunity to join us as subscribers in subsequent seasons. This effort was also motivated by the belief that even though the general public today does not have the interest in classical music that it once did, we still have a responsibility to make it available to all.

Most of the time the strategy worked. Ticket prices were low, and sales to first-time attendees were strong. The venues varied from schools to churches to community centers. The simple fact was that our hall was downtown, in an area that brought fear to the souls of many. Following the notorious Detroit riots of 1967, the population of the city diminished sharply, and safety became a major factor in attracting an audience for decades to follow. Playing concerts in the suburban backyards of former regulars just made sense.

We selected six venues in diverse neighborhoods. Four concerts per year were played in each of these places, and at the end of the third year we added another location. The result was that we now had more than 3,500 new subscribers. Some might argue that four concerts do not make up a series, but in fact many American orchestras offer four, and sometimes even three, concerts in their packaging structure in the main halls.

Because most of the venues could not accommodate the full DSO, we played programs that utilized slightly smaller orchestras. If people wanted to come to hear Mahler, Strauss, a choral work, or one of the top-tier soloists, they would have to go downtown. These neighborhood concerts also provided us with the opportunity to see young up-and-comers, both conductors and soloists alike. I usually did one concert in each venue.

Not all the musicians enjoyed the experience. They did not like being out of Orchestra Hall, and a couple of the performance spaces were physically and acoustically difficult. But after a year or so, it was clearly understood that the more people we attracted, no matter from where, the more financially viable we would become. Also, audiences that simply would not come downtown were now able to enjoy the DSO in their own neighborhoods.

The second of the initiatives that seemed to make a big difference had to do with an idea I had been toying with during the strike. What was really keeping young people from attending symphony concerts? Was it a lack of arts education, no connection to the music, too much competition from other forms of entertainment, a combination of the three, or something else? I put forward another idea.

With the Orchestra Hall audience averaging around 60 percent of capacity, we had plenty of unused inventory. I proposed what eventually would be called a Soundcard. For $25, any student of any age could have unlimited access to all concerts throughout the season in the hall or neighborhood venues. Two weeks prior to the performance, the student could reserve a complimentary ticket with his or her $25 annual membership. After one or two performances, any other events attended were basically free to the cardholders.

"Leonard," some folks said, "are you crazy? This makes no sense financially."

Actually, it did.

In Detroit we knew pretty well in advance how many people were coming to a given event. Our walk-up audience is not large, as many patrons live far away, and we had sophisticated sales-forecasting models at our disposal. So why not use this information to help fill the hall? After all, $25 for each Soundcard is more than we would have received for an empty seat.

The concept took a little while to get legs, but after two seasons we had sold 1,500 Soundcards. That was almost $40,000 in additional revenue. More important, it brought a new, more diverse, and younger audience into Orchestra Hall. If some of these kids were under sixteen years of age, their parents might come as well, paying the regular price for a ticket.

I wondered about the demographic of this young audience. We tried to find out by having a pre-concert talk to which only the Soundcard members were invited. About four hundred people showed up, and it was very clear that many were from minority communities. In particular, I was pleased to see a fairly significant turnout from the Arab population, which is quite large in certain parts of the greater Detroit area.

With the Soundcard in place and the patron-minded pricing structure implemented, we were now looking at houses that were about 92 percent full, a statistic that would be the envy of many orchestras. It did not appear to matter who was playing or what was on the program.

The significant discovery for me was that attracting a younger audience was merely a matter of cutting the price. Of course you must have the quality to back it up, but it seemed that as the orchestra continued to recover from the strike, the audiences also started to grow. And after a while, we were actually presenting more concerts in Orchestra Hall than in any previous season.

Which brings me to what may have been the most important factor in the revival of the DSO—advocating for a somewhat different definition of the word "audience" as it relates to the orchestral world.

In the first quarter of the twenty-first century, we are hearing a lot about the "global audience." People can go to a movie theater and watch a full opera. Museums can display their entire collections online. It is possible that you are reading this via an electronic medium rather than having to physically turn the pages.

The American Federation of Musicians has long stood in the way of reaching new audiences by imposing additional fee requirements for several areas of musical communication. Certainly if we make a recording, as a separate endeavor from a concert, there is a strong argument for further compensation. But if we make our product available to a worldwide audience at no cost to the consumer, why should anyone be paid extra? No additional preparation is involved on the part of the musicians; we are simply doing the same thing we always do.

I found myself trying to convince musicians and board that unless we relaxed the rules, we would continue to limit the number of people who could enjoy what our orchestra produced. Management supported this idea, and the subject was broached during labor negotiations. The musicians and union eventually agreed to a clause in the contract that permitted internet broadcasting of our performances.

Since there was no charge to the public, we needed to identify a funding source. Management and the board went to work quickly, and the project caught the attention of both the Knight and Ford foundations. Between them they contributed almost $1 million toward the production.

At first we were all lost. There were cameras and operators onstage, in the hall, and backstage. There was little if any communication between the control booth and the stagehands. All the presenters seemed ill at ease, and we could not figure out how to fill the time between pieces or during intermission. The resolution of the images was low-definition at best. The audio would go in and out, and often the streaming signal was lost.

Despite a rocky start, the webcasts made an impact immediately. At first we had about a thousand people watching, most in the Detroit area. As word spread about what we were doing, many more tuned in from all over the world. We had viewership for some of the broadcasts that reached more than thirty thousand people. Timing was crucial, as all these events were live. If we had a concert that began at 8:00 p.m. on the East Coast, people in France would have to stay up until 2:00 a.m. to see it. We wound up doing some of these webcasts on our Friday morning or Sunday afternoon performances to make them more accessible to an international audience.

After four years we were still the only orchestra doing anything like this on a regular basis for free. The quality of the sound improved significantly. Thanks to an infusion of funds by a generous donor, we went to high-definition broadcasting, and the bulky cameras and operators involved were replaced by robotics, virtually invisible to anyone who didn't know where they were placed. I started doing intermission interviews with composers and soloists, and we presented additional content and information about the program. We also invited several other Detroit cultural institutions to talk about their own contributions to the city.

When it all began I heard more or less the same question as I did with the Soundcard: "Leonard, are you crazy? Won't this interfere with people actually wanting to attend the live performances?"

In fact, the opposite has been true. As the pooh-bahs in the pop music industry have understood for decades, you utilize one medium to promote another. Not only could the members of our remote audience hear the music, but now they could also begin to identify the musicians visually. Somehow, this made it even more interesting when they came to see us in person. No one I have spoken to has ever said that internet broadcasting kept them from attending a concert, but many have written that they wanted to come to Orchestra Hall as a result.

The next step was to consider how it might be possible to turn this into a revenue-generating effort. I insisted that the live broadcasts of the concerts always be free. However, I supported management's idea to monetize what came to be called DSO Replay. For an annual donation of $50, viewers were given un-limited access to performance webcasts from the previous three years. Almost two hundred works would be made available to enjoy on demand, on any device, seventy-two hours following every live webcast. Again, the cost was minimal, but the result would prove to be more than worthwhile.

With the success of these and other initiatives, we found our-selves thriving. Other orchestras followed our path, developing variations on our model, reaching out to play in surrounding communities, and offering substantial discounts for groups, students, and subscribers.

Taking risks works only if the numbers can back them. What might seem visionary can turn out to be a pipe dream if the whole thing collapses under the weight of economic burden. Many orchestras had become used to a donor simply giving money, without any strings attached. That has changed signifi-cantly over the last twenty years or so. No longer can we solicit funds based on immediate cash needs alone. Rather, we have found it very helpful to involve patrons in projects of particular interest to them.

Fund-raising efforts now also benefit from musicians' being actively involved in virtually every aspect of the organization. The orchestras that will flourish, not just survive, will be those in which a spirit of cooperation and transparency exists. Sometimes I wonder where the DSO would be without that strike. Was it more than just a wakeup call? And would it take repeated crises to keep everyone moving forward?

In the end we have to be equally creative as both fund-raisers and musicians in our ongoing efforts to meet goals of fiscal stability and artistic excellence. In a world whose technologies and community demographics change every day, we cannot stand still.

...AND I'LL HUFF

There is nothing to writing. All you do is sit down at a typewriter and bleed.

—Ernest Hemingway

As social media grew, so did the concept of online journalism. In 2005 Arianna Huffington started what would turn out to be one of the most-read sites on the internet. Contributions to the journal are mostly political in content, but a surprisingly large number of us send in thoughts on the cultural scene. We are limited to about seven hundred words per article.

Here are several of the pieces I have written. With the exception of the first item, an extraordinary story, they are in the order in which they appeared in the *Huffington Post*.

"A Lesson for All"

October 9, 2015

Usually, the first rehearsal for a new season is a straightforward affair. We make announcements, introduce new musicians and staff, and get our collective chops together.

Such was not the case in Detroit on a sunny Thursday morning.

We generally start the season with a series of free concerts throughout the community, made possible by the generous support of the DTE Energy Foundation. The repertoire comprises shorter pieces that we know very well, so the idea is to just play through the works and make a few adjustments as needed. But September 24, 2015, will go down as the most inspirational first rehearsal for the majority of those present in Orchestra Hall.

For the past two years, the DSO staff, board and musicians have participated in a day of service at the Children's Hospital of Michigan. Last fall I had the opportunity to join them, and I stood in admiration of not only these brave patients fighting cancer or other illnesses, but also their caregivers, who completely devote themselves to making positive memories with these children.

Throughout the year, DSO musicians perform in the hospital lobby and provide live music during group sessions alongside such music therapists as Laura Duda, formerly of Children's Hospital of Michigan and now the manager of community engagement for the DSO. Earlier this year, in collaboration with Laura, the DSO began planning an initiative to make our music more accessible to people with special needs. For this first rehearsal, we had made arrangements for approximately twenty such individuals to attend, mostly from Glen Peters School in the Macomb Intermediate School District and the Children's Hospital of Michigan.

The young people who visited us came with parents, teachers, paraprofessionals and friends. Many sat close to the stage. After a few introductory remarks, we began with Leroy Anderson's "Bugler's Holiday." Most of our guests seemed to recognize the sound of the trumpets. Following that, we got everyone involved in the same composer's "Waltzing Cat." It was difficult to tell how many in our audience actually meowed along with the orchestra, but they did laugh when the imitation of a barking dog from three musicians came roaring through at the end.

This past summer, these students from Glen Peters School lost one of their own, a young man named Nathan who was cared for by staff at the Children's Hospital of Michigan. We learned that Nathan loved the tambourine, and two of our percussionists, Joseph Becker and Andrés Pichardo-Rosenthal, came to the front of the stage and demonstrated all the things that this instrument can do. Nathan's parents were in the audience, and we dedicated the rehearsal to the memory of their son as a gesture that we hope provided them some degree of solace.

Next up was the title music from *Star Wars*. At this point, we didn't know how well we were communicating with the young people. However, that all changed with the last selection.

At each of our community concerts, we select a member of the audience to lead "The Stars and Stripes Forever." This time we invited a boy with autism named Connor who, with the help of his father, joined us onstage. When he stepped onto the podium, he was hunched over and clutching a security pillow with both hands.

His dad tried to encourage him to stand up straight, but the boy seemed to retreat. Then I said to Connor that we really wanted him to conduct, and that meant that the orchestra needed to see him. All of a sudden, Connor stood upright and looked for his favorite instrument, the trumpet, played by

Hunter Eberly, who rose to his feet to welcome him. I placed a baton in Connor's hand and showed him how to beat time. Together we gave the downbeat, and the march began.

In view of the consummate joy on this young man's face and the tears coming from members of the orchestra, it's safe to say the sheer realization that music does make a difference has never been so present as it was for these three brief minutes. On his own, Connor released his pillow, dropping it to the floor, and let the sound of the orchestra overtake his entire body. By the time the music ended, we all had been transformed. As musicians, we know that we alter people's lives, but rarely in this palpable way, both in physical and emotional terms.

It was a moment in time that will replay itself over and over in my mind. I am certain that the same thoughts will be in the heads of our musicians. And young Connor, well, we do not know how this experience will affect him. But for a little while, he was the king of the world.

We could not ask for a braver leader.

[A year later Connor returned to Orchestra Hall, baton in hand. We learned that every night he sets up his stuffed animals and leads his orchestra in "The Stars and Stripes Forever."]

"Home, Sweet Homes"

April 9, 2013

The convergence of the Rhône and Saône. Paul Bocuse. The birthplace of cinema. Châteauneuf-du-Pape just a few miles down the road.

It does not get much better than Lyon.

This is the city that I have called my second home for the past two years. Being music director with two orchestras requires a very good set of plans and an even better understanding of the airlines. It also means that I must balance my roles in both Detroit and France.

I am often asked about the differences between the Orchestre National de Lyon and the Detroit Symphony Orchestra. First and foremost is the nature of how each is subsidized. In the States, virtually all the revenue is generated from contributions and ticket sales. Very little comes from local, state or federal funds.

It is quite a different story in Lyon. Even though the orchestra is dubbed "National," the money comes primarily from City Hall. Revenue from the government accounts for perhaps seventy percent of the total budget. People often assume that since the city is footing the majority of the bill, they must be involved in the programming.

To date, there has not been one instance of interference or pressure in any way. Of course I try to promote French composers and performers, but no more so than I do with their American counterparts in Detroit. However, when you have the riches of Berlioz, Debussy, Ravel and Dutilleux, it is a pleasure to place them on concert programs.

Audiences are on the younger side when compared to the States. There is no dress code, and one can see all manner of attire at a performance. In a city of a million and a half residents, probably seven percent attend concerts on a regular basis. In a very successful partnership, the orchestra has paired up with the soccer team, Olympique Lyonnais. Buy a ticket for a match and you get one for a concert. The reverse holds true as well. Imagine that!

The Auditorium is located about a mile from the old part of the city. Across the street is "Les Halles," a most extraordinary marketplace where the great restaurateurs of the city go to claim their fare for the evening. Just seeing the sumptuous layout of quenelles, poularde de Bresse and exquisite cheeses makes one wish that there were rooms available for habitation in the facility.

Like most other orchestras, musicians of the ONL come from different parts of the world, bringing a well-rounded musical profile to the ensemble. But the orchestra is truly French. Their sound comes from a rich tradition of music-making that dominated the landscape for the majority of the twentieth century. The string sound is robust but pure, the woodwinds rich but clear, the brass penetrating but not overwhelming, and the percussion bright and colorful.

The staff is quite a bit smaller than one would find for a similar American ensemble. Concepts of PR, marketing and development are somewhat new, but it is clear that being part of the cultural global market place is important in getting the word out about the city. There is even a campaign called "*Only Lyon*," which is being used to lure companies and tourists to the region.

Working on a regular basis in these two cities, I feel quite fortunate. Although the demands are great, the benefits are enormous. Looking out of my apartment window and seeing the gently flowing Rhône, I can only think, "Quand le vin est tiré, il faut le boire." (When the wine is drawn, one must drink.)

"How Do You Get to Carnegie Hall?"

May 3, 2013

On the corner of 57th Street and 7th Avenue sits the most famous concert hall in the world. No less a figure than Tchaikovsky led the first performances in 1891. Virtually every major artist has performed there.

There is simply no place like it.

The first time I stepped foot in Carnegie Hall was in 1964. I was a student at the Juilliard School and had bought a ticket to what I thought was going to be a performance of music by Benjamin Britten. It turned out that I did not check the date and wound up at a Beethoven recital by Wilhelm Backhaus.

You feel the sense of history upon entering the hall. The horseshoe shape makes it seem larger than life and perhaps it is. In those days, the sound was rich, warm and like velvet. It covered up many sins and in some cases made the musicians sound better than they were. And of course the great ones were made even more astonishing.

I listened to Horowitz, Heifetz, Rubinstein, and Fischer-Dieskau. The orchestras from Chicago, Philadelphia, Cleveland, Berlin and Vienna were regular visitors. Jazz and pop music were also part of the agenda with concerts by Sinatra, Brubeck and Streisand very much on my radar.

In 1965 I stepped onto the stage for the first time. My debut was with the New York Youth Symphony Orchestra, and we played a piece by William Schuman. On that occasion I thought the hall must have seated 15,000 people, so overwhelming was the perspective from the podium. The ghosts of the greats haunted the dressing room, and it was with a certain amount of fear that I walked to the center of the platform.

A very kind attendant said something that perhaps allayed some of my trepidations. "You know, there have been numerous concerts here, some good and some bad. Just enjoy the moment."

And I did.

Over the years it has been my privilege to lead performances with St. Louis, the National Symphony, Cleveland Orchestra and so many other wonderful organizations. Now, I will bring my Detroit Symphony to Carnegie, the first time in seventeen years for the orchestra. We will perform two concerts with vastly different repertoire.

Two years ago, the hall started a project called "Spring for Music." The idea was to present a week of programs featuring orchestras that have innovative concepts. The first of ours, on Thursday, May 9, will feature music by Rachmaninoff, Weill, and Ravel, composers who had to come to grips with creating music in the twentieth century, even though their musical leanings tended to reflect a nineteenth-century aesthetic.

The second program, on Friday, May 10, will comprise the four numbered symphonies by Charles Ives, the first time this has ever been done. Over the course of twenty years or so, the composer can be seen as a naïve and somewhat amateur creator, eventually emerging as the most original force in American music. The world premieres of his second and fourth symphonies were given in Carnegie, and I was actually in attendance for the latter in 1965.

There will be almost a thousand people coming from Detroit to hear us in New York, yet another sign of the continued growth of the artistic culture in the Motor City. Hopefully we will look and sound distinct, with a musical profile that makes this trip special for our own audience as well as those from New York.

And the answer to the title question? Practice, practice, practice! Oh, and when we leave the hotel, we make a left and go two blocks.

"What Would Roger Ebert Think?"

June 17, 2013

"Look! Up on the screen! Is it a bird? Is it a plane? It's the *Man of Steel*!"

How times have changed. Superman is no longer in the title. The campy, mild-mannered reporter is nowhere to be found. Lois Lane does not spend a whole film trying to figure out who he is. You cannot go out whistling any of the tunes, as there are none.

Our icons from the past have been undergoing severe transformations. Perhaps the younger generation is more clued in to these darker versions of superheroes, but I miss the humor and

whimsy that made them endearing. Now the Batmen, Spider-
men and Supermen each have troubled pasts and spend a great
deal of time on the cinematic therapist's couch. This is the new
role assigned to the moviegoer.

Each of the main characters has serious family issues. The recent incarnation of the indestructible one abandons the tights,
the yellow in the insignia, and pretty much his sense of humor.
Not that the new film is bad. The first hour or so gives some
real heft to the background story. Newcomers to the saga, if
there are any, will learn that our hero is called Kal, rather than
his full name of Kal-El. That only comes into play when we
need to know more about his relationship to his father. Since
we do not see the name in print, it is possible to surmise that it
is spelled Cal, giving the young man a trendy moniker.

Remember the days when we sat by the television to watch
the weekly excursions of George Reeves? Remember the theme
music? Or the Christopher Reeve versions with one of John
Williams' memorable marches?

Those days have gone by faster than a speeding bullet. Yes, the
recent scores are great for the chases and fight sequences. And it
is certainly loud enough. I thought that the *Transformers* films had
set the limit, but there seems to be no end to the decibel levels in
today's movie marketplace. *Spinal Tap* would have to give it a 12.

Just as we want to have memorable screen personalities, so
we want music to match. Action sagas are a little like Wagner or
Puccini operas, in which the characters have leitmotifs not only
on stage but in the pit as well. Wouldn't it be nice to have snippets
of identifying music played when the protagonist is young and

only have a full statement of the tune when he or she has matured? Even sub-themes for the villains would give us aural clues as well as visual ones, allowing the director, producer and composer to create a more integrated experience.

Mind you, I am not criticizing the creators of these scores. They are doing their best to engage the viewer, without drawing undue attention to the soundtrack. Composers must walk a fine line between overstatement and understatement. There are even times when silence is the best score of all, especially when tension is called for.

Summer was meant for these types of movies, although I am not sure how many visions of the apocalypse we really need to see. For now, Metropolis is only somewhat damaged as well as a few patrons' eardrums. There are not many buildings left to bound over. They will certainly be rebuilt in time for the sequel.

We wish Superman luck in his pursuit of truth, justice and a proper theme song.

"Stars and Stripes Forever?"

July 2, 2013

Get out the hot dogs, flags and stereos. July 4th is upon us, and once again the musical forces of the United States will be in full sway. Patriotic concerts will take place from sea to shining sea, and audiences will flock to hear that most American of pieces, Tchaikovsky's *1812 Overture*. Huh?

Yes, this piece, celebrating Napoleon's retreat from Russia, has become the unofficial anthem of our most celebrated celebration. The public would forgo Sousa, John Williams and Gershwin, but take away Pyotr Ilyich and all muskets would break out.

Surprisingly, Fourth of July concerts were not always filled with fireworks and cannon barrages. It was not until the 1970s, when Boston Pops conductor Arthur Fiedler decided to introduce live cannon fire into the concert proceedings that the idea took off. And of course this was at a time when there were still Soviets.

Never mind that the work incorporates music from Russian liturgy. Never mind that the main tune at the end is "God Save the Tsar." Never mind that the only other national anthem heard is "La Marseillaise." No, that does not stop culture-hungry Americans from thinking that this piece is all ours.

How come we don't have the "1776 Overture"? Certainly there must be some good tunes from back then that all of us can recognize? Or is it not a case of the music itself?

Fiedler was quite savvy when it came to understanding his audience. He knew that they wanted something showy, and the Tchaikovsky was already well known through recordings. Some of those incorporated the cannon fire, and all that needed to be done was to add it to our own revolutionary celebration. The idea stuck, and it is not to be undone.

I have led these concerts in many cities, not all of them in the United States. Europeans really don't have an equivalent in terms of concerts that commemorate historical events. The closest would be in London, for the Last Night of the Proms. The final thirty minutes or so consists of patriotic British music, with the audience dressed in all kinds of attire. They bring klaxons, flags and any accouterments they can think of to join in the merriment. It is all great fun but often leads to charges of jingoism. There are those who want to get rid of the patriotic element altogether, but after 110 years or so, that is not going to happen.

In France, Bastille Day goes by somewhat quietly. Orchestras do not participate because they are on vacation. Of course there is May Day in Russia, where they do not play the *1812 Overture*.

Back in the States, we will continue to present our Fourth of July concerts. Some will be televised and might feature major stars from recordings, Broadway and film. Others will be low key, with perhaps a small group of musicians in a park. We have a few traditions besides Tchaikovsky. Certainly the National Anthem will be played, as well as some Sousa marches. Members of the military will be recognized.

But people will still flock because of the Russian bombast. Maybe the best way to Americanize the work is to change the name of the composer to John Philip Tchaikovsky. And if the piece is really an overture, perhaps we should play it at the start of the concert.

We rightfully love our traditions, even though they are sometimes borrowed. This nation of immigrants includes not only the people but the music as well.

"Orchestra Moving to the Internet"

November 26, 2013

The most important question American orchestras face is: How do we reach new audiences? You all know the complaints:

> "The average age of the audience is increasing."
> "Classical music has little relevance today."
> "The economic market cannot sustain an orchestra."

The list goes on, but in my hometown, we have found a way to buck the trend.

After a six-month strike, during which many in the industry wrote off the Detroit Symphony Orchestra as yet another casualty in the Motor City, we have bounced back with new initiatives that have helped to address these concerns.

One method in particular has been a boon for us: Internet broadcasting of virtually all of our subscription concerts. As a result of cooperation among the musicians, board, union and management, a deal was reached that allows this to occur with very little outlay from cash resources. Through the generous support of the Ford Motor Company Fund and The John S. and James L. Knight Foundation, and in collaboration with Detroit Public Television, we have been able to reach thousands of viewers around the world, most of whom previously did not know about the DSO.

In my mind, much of the forward thinking has to do with the realization that the definition of the word "audience" has changed, at least for this orchestra. No longer does it consist of just those people who come to Orchestra Hall, but it now includes music lovers in homes, hospitals and even automobiles. Clearly, this is a throwback to the days when people would tune in, for example, on Sundays to listen to broadcasts by the New York Philharmonic. As a youngster growing up in Los Angeles, this was my audio window to a special musical world. Being able to listen with my family was very special indeed.

How does this new technology help solve the so-called crisis?

Clearly, the age of this audience is mostly younger. We know this through the comments we receive each week. They love not only the programs but also the additional content. Sometimes we feature voiceovers about the music to be heard; other times we present interviews with the artists or composers. We also give them a few glimpses into the diverse arts scene in the Detroit metro area. Last year, I was able to have a friendly web competition with Michael Tilson Thomas as to whose baseball team would win the World Series.

A few weeks ago, we presented the American premiere of *Cyborg* by the Barcelona-based composer Ferran Cruxient. He was not able to make it out to Detroit for the performance, but he watched, via internet, with his father, to whom the work is dedicated, from his home. I gave him a cyberspace bow.

For Thanksgiving week, we will present the world premiere of David Del Tredici's only opera, *Dum Dee Tweedle*. Although we expect good attendance at home, most others, including journalists, cannot attend. But many will be watching from their own base of operations, and a few will actually review the concert, covering not only the musical content, but the televised quality as well.

Because the idea seemed so unique and relevant, we have been able to secure the needed funds that allow us to do these broadcasts. It does not put very much money into anyone's pockets, as the proceeds mostly go towards the production costs. Starting in January, we will have robotic cameras, which will provide us with more flexibility in the way viewers will see the orchestra.

After two years of these webcasts, we are still learning what works and what does not. Most of the time we get it right. As with any live television event, there are moments of fragility, but these are offset by the sheer joy of each concert. We are building our audience on a worldwide scale yet continue to reach those who come—week in, week out—to experience the marvelous acoustics of Orchestra Hall.

Who knows what the next development with the global audience will be?

"Vive la Différence"

February 18, 2014

They come in all shapes and sizes. They range in age. Their dress can vary from jeans to tuxedoes. The audience for classical music has always been somewhat diverse in appearance and appreciation. I am often asked about the differences in Europe, Asia and the United States when it comes to reactions from the public.

This question came to mind recently when I conducted two concerts with my orchestra from Lyon. On a Thursday night, we played an all-Russian program at home, and the next evening we repeated the same concert in Grenoble, a little more than an hour's drive away. The audience in Lyon varied in age and dressed mostly casually. The crowd to the southeast was quite a bit older and came in suits.

Both groups loved the concert. There were demands for an encore from the soloist. Not too much coughing occurred, even though it was the middle of February and there was a lot of quiet music being played. So to me, the two audiences seemed mostly similar. However, there was a distinct disparity when it came to the form of appreciation shown to the artists at the end of their performances.

In Lyon, when the public enjoys the concert, around the third curtain call they begin a rhythmic clapping. It seems to be spontaneous, but I always wonder how they know when to start and what tempo it will be. Somehow the audience members have the identical metronome mark within them, and this form of applause lasts for quite some time. It is not like the sometimes half-hearted attempts to start "The Wave" at sports events.

In Grenoble there was no sign of this ensemble clapping. Applause was more than generous, but the imitation of a drum corps was nowhere to be found. This city, which like Lyon hosted the Olympics, is in the same region as our home, the Rhône Alpes. So it would seem that there would be little difference in local characteristics. Not having time to explore the city, I know nothing about the customs in Grenoble. But certainly they do not behave the same as their compatriots from Lyon.

And so I began to ponder other differentiations in audience behavior. For the most part, Asian and European audiences do not head for the doors at the end of a concert in what is sometimes described as a "walking ovation." This practice seems reserved for the States. Whistling as a sign of appreciation is a definite no-no, as it is equated with booing. Although whistling is acceptable at rock concerts and jazz presentations, the classical etiquette demands a slightly more sedate set of responses.

One thing seems universal: audiences are not always sure when to clap. Even in the great European capitals, one can encounter applause between movements or, in the case of Tchaikovsky's 5th Symphony, during the finale. I remember a case at the Hollywood Bowl when we were performing the First Violin Concerto by Shostakovich. There is a long and brilliant cadenza between the third and fourth movements. The orchestra signals the end of the violinist's turn, and at that time, the audience erupted as if a fantastic drum solo in a club had just occurred.

The question of when to applaud is hotly debated in musical circles. Some say that it must only come at the end of a complete piece, lest the atmosphere be ruined. Of course this is mitigated by the same people who have no problem with outbursts at the end of arias in an opera, thereby completely disturbing the flow of the story. No one applauds at the end of a Hamlet soliloquy, so why do it in the opera house? When is the last time you actually heard the last few measures of the first act of *La Bohème*?

But who can resist bursting out with enthusiasm when a great performance of the first movement of the Paganini First Violin Concerto or Rachmaninov Second Piano Concerto has occurred? For me, it really is a matter of allowing audiences the opportunity to express themselves and perhaps relieve some of the tension that has occurred in the music before the commencement of the next movement. After all, if they do not applaud, they most certainly will cough, and that is actually worse.

As Manny Ax so succinctly put it, "Applause should be an emotional response to the music rather than a regulated social duty."

"That Other Musical Minority"

March 11, 2014

As I was writing a chapter for a forthcoming book about the music profession, I thought about all the barriers that have been broken and those yet to be breached. My focus was on females, African Americans and homosexuals. But while putting the words down, I was reminded of a conversation I had with the Detroit Symphony Assistant Conductor, Teddy Abrams. We were discussing the building of a career for the young maestro, who was about to be appointed music director of the Louisville Symphony.

Teddy pointed out something that had not occurred to me before. Virtually no American orchestras were engaging guest conductors from our own country under the age of forty-five.

For the most part, aside from a few assistant conductorships, the younger generation of maestros is primarily limited to musicians from other countries. And at that, forty-five may not be considered so young.

A little research proved Teddy correct. Although there were a few exceptions, most orchestras did not engage the younger Americans at all, and only a couple of groups had even one on the subscription season. Why this struck me as unusual was that not so long ago many of us were directing the most important ensembles as guest conductors at an early stage in our careers.

Just think about this list: James Levine, James Conlon, Michael Tilson Thomas, David Zinman, André Previn, Gerard Schwarz, Lawrence Foster, Dennis Russell Davies and myself, among many others, were regularly present on almost every orchestra's podiums. And we all did this well before the forty-five-year-old barrier.

Nowadays it is impossible to witness the equivalent. Although there has been an increase in the number of younger conductors gracing American podiums, very few of them come from within the country. Much used to be made of who would be the next Bernstein. Several of us succeeded in forging careers, and of course, many others went by the wayside. But the opportunities were there.

What has happened? Were we that much better than the young Americans of today? Is the attraction of a foreign accent still in play?

Mind you, I am certainly no fan of the quota system when it comes to musical decisions. We must all be measured by the quality of what we produce. And I am as guilty as the next music director when it comes to unintentionally excluding the junior American maestros. For nine years I trained many during an annual course in Washington. I also see several each year in various cities.

What can or should be done?

For starters, just simple awareness might help. With all the attention focused on other minorities in our profession, perhaps it is also time to include another category. In much the same way as we choose to promote women and others in the field, perhaps it is also time to consider our own homegrown talent. Naturally each and every orchestra must select those who are considered ready for the big push and musically strong enough to lead those ensembles.

Much of the responsibility will fall to two people: the music director and the artistic administrator. The former rarely has the opportunity to see other conductors, but the latter is able to travel about, scouting the best new talent. There is also the possibility that members of a given orchestra might have worked with one of the young podium minders and been impressed. That was actually how Teddy was recommended to the Detroit Symphony.

It is still not an easy path. Nothing is as valuable as hard work, and no one should be afforded an engagement simply based on how he or she looks or where he or she is from. But some encouragement for the new kids on the block is important. We must not leave the younger generation of American conductors behind.

"Where Did Our Musical Legacy Go?"

March 18, 2014

Several months ago, I wrote on this site about the lack of younger American talent on the podiums of major orchestras in the United States. Since there are still a couple of ensembles that have not yet announced their 2014–15 season plans, the follow-up article is still in limbo.

While I was looking at not only the artists, but the programming as well, an astonishing statistic jumped out at me. With the exception of the five usual suspects, almost every orchestra I delved into was completely devoid of most composers who laid the foundations for symphonic music in our country.

First, a bit of background. I perused the season announcements of the fifteen orchestras with the largest budgets, only taking into account subscription concerts. Then I divided the American composers into two groups, those living and those deceased. The good news is that those still among us are fairly well represented these days. Out of the orchestras surveyed, five of them were scheduled to perform more than five works by composers active today. In some cases, when a composer has a relationship with a specific orchestra, there are several works by that person within the season. There remains one orchestra that is not playing even one work by any American on its subscription season.

Then came the bad news. Yes, we see a bit of Ives, Gershwin, Copland and Bernstein, and several orchestras are doing the

Barber Violin Concerto. But after that, you have to look very hard to find anyone else represented from our rich classical music heritage. Four of the orchestras are not even performing one work from this canon.

America was one of the last countries to embrace the literal symphonic tradition in the 20th century. Composers such as William Schuman, Walter Piston, Roy Harris, Peter Mennin, Roger Sessions, Vincent Persichetti and so many others made vital contributions to this country's culture. Virtually every orchestra and conductor, regardless of the nationality of the music director, performed their music.

How is it possible to ignore musical luminaries such as David Diamond, Lukas Foss, Howard Hanson, Virgil Thompson or the dozens of others who meant so much to this country's landscape? Aside from the occasional festival, which might try to resurrect some of these composers for one-off performances, it is doubtful that even music students today know their names.

One of the questions I am often asked by aspiring maestros is, "How can I attract attention to my conducting?" My answer is quite simple: "Find a repertoire that is unique to you while you are studying the classics."

It would not be fair of me to speak on behalf of other conductors, but when I was starting out, I made a conscious decision to lead works by American composers, both living and deceased. There were not many others out there doing this repertoire at the time, and it provided me with ample opportunity to bring attention to both the music and myself. To this day, I and a very few of my peers continue to present some of these scores to orchestras and the public. Certainly it is fine to have fresh takes on Beethoven, Strauss, Bartók and all the others who are performed regularly. But it takes a great deal more work, research and study to find those pieces that can help put a conductor on the musical map.

Whether we look at the pre-Ivesian composers, the eccentrics, the neo-romantics and impressionists, or the edgy and innovative composers, America has had a lot to say in the world of classical music. It is an embarrassment and a shame that we are in danger of losing these traditions. Performances can no longer be left to just those of us who grew up with this music. We will not be here that much longer. New talent has an obligation to seek out what made this country culturally strong.

One of the paths to the future involves traveling on older roads. Sometimes they lead to great discoveries.

"The Wait Is Not Over"

May 5, 2014

Every one of us has had the following experience:

All of our lines are busy. Please hold for the next available agent. All calls will be answered in the order received.

It is certainly possible that the operators are speaking with other customers, and perhaps there really are thousands of people sitting around waiting to speak with someone. There is nothing that we can do about that.

Of course, each company has a different method of dealing with this period of time. Some tell you how long it will be before a live person will speak with you. Others just let the line go silent. Various advertisements for other products by the corporation can also be heard.

But there is one item that we, the public, can insist on: quality control over the music that is played while holding.

Over at my telephone/internet/cable company, they play one lite jazz segment over and over. I know this because there was a problem with iTunes downloading, so I called my service provider. For more than an hour I listened to this ditty, all thirty seconds of it, repeated and repeated. It was minimalist hell. If I put the phone on mute, I would not know if an operator really was standing by.

Does each of these firms have a music department? Is there someone in charge who asks, "What can we do to annoy our customers even further?" The others at the corporate table chime in with suggestions, each designed to make the caller frustrated at every turn.

Then the music supervisor says, "I know. Let's find the most innocuous and least offensive recording possible. It needs to be just a bit catchy at first, with a little backbeat, but after that, it will cause our clients to be obsessed with the waiting period. In other words, we dare them to stick it out."

"But what if we lose subscribers?"

"Then they will learn how much worse our competitors are."

The decision on what style of music to play must rest with someone. Perhaps that person should be forced to sit in a chair and listen to this piece for an hour or so, just as I did. In that time, even if they are not trained musicians, they will have enough time to take the notes down and transcribe the whole thing for symphonic band.

What can we do?

Our first hurdle is getting to a live person to explain our frustration. So I suggest that when you actually speak with someone, get a better phone number that will connect you directly, rather than having to wade through the menu. Distribute this to your friends and contacts. After that, it is only a matter of time before one of us figures out who is in charge of the holding pattern.

Here are the pieces of music that I think should be playing for this time period. If the wait will be five minutes, we should be able to listen to Dave Brubeck's "Take Five." Ten minutes can be assigned to Bob Dylan's "Desolation Row." Anything longer must be Terry Riley's *In C*—simply because the music, like the wait, can go on indefinitely.

Maybe there could be a personalized menu that would allow callers to decide what kind of music they would prefer.

All operators are busy. What would you like to hear? Press 1 for Classical, 2 for Jazz, 3 for Rock, 4 for Country, 5 for Heavy Metal, 6 for Gospel, 7 for Sinatra, or 8 for New Age. Press 0 if you prefer "The Sounds of Silence."

One final thought: Are there royalty distributions for usage of copyrighted material via telephone? If there are, I suggest that you propose to your provider that my recording of Copland's "Hoedown" is the perfect way to spend all that time. If enough of you do that, it is very possible that I may never have to use a phone again, since there will be no service on my remote island in the South Pacific.

WHAT'S NEWS?

Every actor in his heart believes everything bad that's printed about him.

—Orson Welles

Critics. The people musicians love to hate. Those who write about us seem to have unlimited power to make or break careers. Sometimes the concertgoing public waits to have its own thoughts either validated or repudiated following a performance. Very few of us take the time to understand what the critic really does and how it can impact the musical world.

This chapter attempts to shed some light on the profession of music journalism from a conductor's point of view. There is no need to go into the history of criticism; that has been done over and over. Still, it is always instructive to look at Nicolas Slonimsky's *Lexicon of Musical Invective* to see where the pundits got it wrong.

One of the questions that most musicians are asked is, "Do you read your own reviews?" Pretty much from the time I started garnering reviews, I devoured them. But there are examples of conductors who request that any references to their work in the press first be cut out of the newspaper before they read the remaining portions of the review.

For conductors and, indeed, all musicians, reviews can be important for several reasons. At the top of the list is that they can promote a career. If a highly favorable article appears, this might help secure an agent, a recording contract, and other benefits.

Critics are pretty much everywhere. Influential donors, individual ticket buyers, and the musicians one leads put the conductor under the microscope. The court of public opinion can turn a vision into a nightmare and vice versa. It can also change the way a conductor approaches music making and the repertoire he or she chooses to perform.

What is the role of the critic? First and foremost, I believe that he or she should be a reporter, charged with telling the readership what occurred at any given musical event. Too often the journalist does not say, for example, how many people attended a concert, how the public responded to the performers, or how the consensus might have differed from the critic's own opinion. One of the oft-heard phrases from the Monday-morning quarterbacks is: "The writer must have gone to a different concert than I did."

What qualifies a critic for the job? Although it is not necessary to have been a performing musician or composer, it does help to have more than just a listener's point of view.

What challenges do critics face? In a city such as London, the job is particularly difficult. With five full-time symphony orchestras, two opera companies, and myriad smaller ensembles, critics are expected to know and write about everything. Also, with all that activity, they hear the same pieces often and have to find different ways to describe the same music they might have heard just a few weeks earlier.

Once upon a time every newspaper had a large staff of people writing about music because there were so many concerts on any given night. Today things are different. It is not that there are fewer performances, but there are not as many print papers as there used to be. Arts coverage has been drastically cut by editors, usually for budgetary reasons, and many events pass unnoticed. The debut recital of a young artist, unless it is in one of the big halls, usually goes unmentioned.

Even the recording industry has been affected by this reduction in arts journalism. There are fewer publications devoted to reviewing music. And the newest form of commercial release, the stream or download of classical music, is mostly ignored.

We know that a review can help or ruin a film, Broadway show, or opera production. In the old days reviews appeared the day after the performance. If the event was to recur over several weeks, the review either helped to generate ticket sales or might even shut the whole production down. The same could not be said for orchestral events. Sometime during the 1980s newspapers began delaying the reviews for two days, and by the time readers got around to seeing what the critics thought, the program had ended its run.

Many people are surprised to learn that most of the time the person writing the review is not the one who pens the headline. This applies not only to the arts but to virtually every aspect of newspaper policy. That boldfaced item is the one meant to get you to read the whole article.

And of course, space limitations make a full accounting of an event impossible at times. Whole portions of a performance may be eliminated or reduced to one sentence. This is when the bias of the critic comes into play. If the writer loves new music, as much as three-quarters of the review will be about that work, even if it occupies the shortest amount of time on the program. Yet there are often people in attendance hearing all of the music for the first time, and they, in particular, would benefit from commentary on every piece.

Occasionally, critics venture too far off base and find themselves in trouble. Such was the case with Frank Peters when he wrote an article, unrelated to me, with the headline: "Can You Hear the Difference?" On January 16, 1982, we were treated to this in the *Post-Dispatch*:

> Are black voices different from white voices? A lot of people, including black singers, think there is a distinctive racial quality, something in the sound of the singing voice, that goes beyond acquired habits of speech. Harold C. Schonberg takes up the old question today toward the end of a *New York Times* article about the progress of black opera singers in the last twenty-seven years.

Later in the piece, we learn of one of the most bizarre experiments ever conducted in the musical field:

> We decided to carry out . . . a test, using taped excerpts from records old and recent, and asking listeners to write on a

numbered list which singers they thought were black. Sixteen voices were judged by fourteen people, all of them white. Six of the judges are professional or advanced student singers: six others work elsewhere in the music field and hear singers often: a housewife and a teen-age rock consumer were added as controls.

Many of us wrote to the paper insisting on the journalist's removal, to which the *Post* promptly agreed.

Now it is time to get into the good, the bad, and the ugly regarding my personal relationships with critics.

Let's start at the beginning.

After conducting various school and youth orchestras, my first position was as assistant conductor of the St. Louis Symphony. At the time, there were two newspapers in town, the *St. Louis Post-Dispatch* and the *St. Louis Globe-Democrat*. The first article about me appeared on July 29, 1968, in the *Post*. The author was the aforementioned Frank Peters, a sports columnist turned music critic. The piece included the usual background material, but this sentence stood out and was surprisingly perceptive: "Slatkin has generally conservative musical and personal tastes."

My first actual review came out on October 14, 1968, for a concert that fell in a new series of light classics that I started called the Sunday Festival of Music. This time the critic was one Richard Hirsh writing for the *St. Louis Post-Dispatch*:

Slatkin conducts with rather fluid motions, and this seems to
leave the orchestra lacking a certain amount of rhythmic
support, as in the Mahler piece [the Adagietto from the Fifth
Symphony]. Also, Slatkin uses very steady tempoes [sic]; this
tended to detract from Mahler, certain parts of *Till Eulenspiegel*,
and from the waltzes. These last were growing tedious toward
the end of the program, because there was little variation in
the tastefully subdued oom-pahs.

Not the greatest start for my first real job, but probably all
true. I chose a program that was difficult to pull off with one
rehearsal, and I was more than likely a little tentative throughout.

During my twenty-seven years in St. Louis, the vast majority
of reviews were favorable, helping build audiences, with only
the occasional complaint regarding my repertoire choices.
There seemed to be no question that the orchestra became an
important force on the orchestral map. Subscriptions increased,
but we still had deficits almost every year. The fact that not only
the local critics, but also those on a national level, pointed to our
growth made for one of the best music stories in the country.

In 1983 *Time* magazine's Michael Walsh declared the St. Louis
Symphony "the second-best orchestra" in the United States,
just behind Chicago. Of course, we milked that for all it was
worth. Other publications picked up on the article, and suddenly
we were in demand everywhere.

The timing could not have been better for me. The next year
we won our first Grammy Award for a recording of Prokofiev's
Fifth Symphony. Our annual trips to Carnegie Hall were much

anticipated because we brought very unusual repertoire to New York. Whether because of William Bolcom's *Songs of Innocence and of Experience*, Max Davies's *Worldes Blis*, Nick Maw's *Odyssey*, or any number of other pieces heard in Manhattan for the first time, houses were full, and reviews contained high praise.

Back home there started to be rumblings of discontent. Some members of the board were getting a bit annoyed with the programming. After seventeen years as the orchestra's music director, it was time for me to move on. Even though the relatively new critic, James Wierzbicki, felt that I should have been more profound, he generally was favorable, as this piece in the February 27, 1994 edition of the *Post-Dispatch* suggests:

> Season after season he has guided the orchestra through effective performances in East Coast music centers, and month after month he's done the same thing in Powell Hall. . . . Slatkin is hardly a superficial conductor; at the same time, he seldom manages to dig very deep into the scores he addresses.

His successor, only for the final six months of my tenure, was not so generous. The name Philip Kennicott, who later won a Pulitzer Prize, will come up a few more times over the course of this chapter. For a story in *Nashville Scene* that ran on July 12, 2007, he contributed this statement:

> For me the big question isn't what happened to Slatkin but what happened to that entire generation of American conductors?

Maybe it's because of the decline of the classical record industry, or maybe it's been the shortage of important posts, but with the exception of [San Francisco Symphony music director] Michael Tilson Thomas, the conductors of Slatkin's generation—Andrew Litton, Hugh Wolff, and I think even Marin Alsop—have all failed to achieve a comfortable mature period.

Everyone is entitled to his or her opinion, but each of us mentioned in the article tried to do something important for American musical culture, sacrificing some of the tried-and-true while expanding awareness in new areas. It is not that we were hacks when it came to the core repertoire, but rather that we each made our marks in individual ways.

Early in my career, I had a string of successes as a last-minute replacement for conductors who were unable to fulfill their commitments. It was 1974, the year I broke through.

First up was the New York Philharmonic:

He conducted Mr. Muti's original program with professional aplomb and made a considerable splash at times with Proko-fiev's Symphony No. 5.

—Donal Henahan, *New York Times*, January 12, 1974

After that I made a guest appearance in Chicago, which at the time had four major dailies. "Slatkin's skill catches the upbeat," read the headline in the *Chicago Tribune* on April 6, 1974. "A thousand welcomes to Leonard Slatkin, who began what could be a long and rewarding musical life in this city," wrote Karen Monson of the *Chicago Daily News*. As Robert C. Marsh penned in the *Chicago Sun Times*, "He has at twenty-nine all the skills and all the qualities of leadership necessary to win the respect of a great orchestra and have them play for him with enthusiasm and the fullest measure of their talent." Finally, Roger Dettmer of *Chicago Today* called me "the finest yet of the young American conductors heard downtown . . . more than just talented."

I was on cloud ten. Part of this success had to do with the fact that I chose a program that was very unusual, with works by Purcell (arranged by Britten), Vaughan Williams, Walter Piston, and Maurice Ravel, with three pieces that had never been played by the CSO. This concept of bringing nontraditional works to orchestras would become a signature of mine and eventually caused a bit of a backlash.

It went on this way for most of my debuts over the next several years, whether in the United States or abroad. With the St. Louis Symphony going on tour to Europe and Asia, again with slightly unusual repertoire, the journalists continued to generate positive press. But some were starting to wonder if I was limiting myself:

> Slatkin was a great technician and a quick study, and I admired the way he could effortlessly learn a new and complicated score. My problem with Slatkin was a lack of depth. I was looking for performances, especially of the core repertoire, that seemed deeply considered over a lifetime, and I wasn't getting that from him.

Thus spake Philip Kennicott in the aforementioned interview for *Nashville Scene* in 2007. And he was not the only one expressing reservations. Some saw me as a specialist, in particular of American, British, and Russian music. This was during the time when most orchestras in the United States were focusing on the Austro-German repertoire. I was now considered an anomaly.

After the lengthy stay in St. Louis, it was time to move on. President Bill Clinton came to a performance I did as a guest conductor in Washington, D.C., and said he hoped I would become the next music director of the National Symphony. It was an offer I could not refuse.

It was my belief that the orchestra of the nation's capital should be reflective of American culture, which meant ignoring the criticisms that were starting to come my way. Not that I avoided the standard repertoire, but at that point Washingtonians seemed tired of all the Russian music performed by my predecessor, Mstislav Rostropovich.

The chief critic in Washington was Tim Page. I knew him from a visit he had made to St. Louis. In a profile of me on September 13, 1996, for the *Washington Post*, Page wrote: "Last night, a few minutes after 8:30, Leonard Slatkin, the new music director of the National Symphony Orchestra, walked onto the podium of the Kennedy Center Concert Hall, lifted his baton, and embarked upon an experiment that is certain to challenge—and perhaps fundamentally change—the time-honored role of an orchestra in the United States."

The years passed, and most of the time it was my feeling that Tim got it right, even when being negative about certain performances. Tim was in London on the day of the 9/11 attacks. The two of us spent that evening at a restaurant discussing with other patrons how the world had changed. After a brief retirement from the *Post*, Tim came back, but his opinions of my work had changed, as revealed in this story from August 29, 2004:

> Slatkin's taste in contemporary music is unreliable: He generally shies away from distinctly original new work and leans toward a sort of eclectic pastiche. Moreover, some of the American composers of the recent past he has championed—Samuel Barber, William Schuman, the symphonic Bernstein—are beginning to seem as overrated today as they may have been underrated when Slatkin started putting them on his programs. Then there are times when one senses that Slatkin is more interested in making "news"—The Beethoven "Tenth"! A Percussion Festival! —than he is in exploring the deepest recesses of the repertory's masterpieces. When listening to Gustav Mahler's much-touted (by Slatkin) arrangements of Beethoven's symphonies last season, one felt that the younger composer's amendments both bloated and depleted the originals. At best, they were novelties; at worst, desecrations.

For my sixtieth birthday concert in Washington, a host of great artists was invited to participate. I had no knowledge of who was going to be there until two days before the event. Included in the group were violinists Midori, Joshua Bell, Itzhak Perlman, Pinchas Zukerman, and Elmar Oliveira. The flutist James Galway

was on hand, as were the piano-duo sisters Katia and Marielle
Labèque. John Williams made an appearance, and so did Emanuel
Ax, Jean-Yves Thibaudet, Jeffrey Siegel, Joseph Kalichstein, and
Peter Schickele. The whole thing was the best birthday bash one
could imagine. However, Tim did not think so, as he expressed
in this *Washington Post* review, published September 27, 2004:

> For better and for worse, the evening was Slatkin all over.
> There was variety and humor, there were fancy guests (albeit
> the same ones who always seem to drop in at Slatkin's place).
> There was showbiz galore (complete with spoken testa-
> ments), there was some solid (and some sloppy) playing
> from the NSO. And finally—no way around it—there was a
> certain innate tastelessness to the whole endeavor. Rarely
> have so many talented people come together to produce an
> evening with such a paucity of memorable music. If no other
> conductor could have produced such a show, very few other
> conductors would have permitted it.

During his short retirement from the *Post*, Tim had relin-
quished his chief critic duties—to Philip Kennicott. Mind you, I
have no problem with anyone who writes an opinion, whether
pro or con. It is their job, and there was no question that Kennicott was a fine writer. But sometimes, not often, facts are so
misunderstood, misstated, or just plain wrong that it is not
possible to stay silent.

For the turn of the millennium, I wanted three living American composers, including Joan Tower and Richard Danielpour,

to share the evening. Two of the pieces on the program would receive their world premieres. The third composer being featured was Michael Kamen, best known for his work in film. Here are a few observations by Kennicott, writing in the *Washington Post* on January 14, 2000:

> Last night, the National Symphony Orchestra offered nothing but weeds and garbage, music that doesn't belong in a concert hall, music that adds nothing to our understanding of the sentiments it strives to depict, music that has little use of any kind. It was two hours of despair and perhaps the worst single evening at the Kennedy Center Concert Hall this season.

It did not end there. As various journalists were asked to single out the most significant event that honored the millennium, Kennicott continued his rant on December 31, 2000, almost a year after the premiere:

> Barely two weeks into the new year the National Symphony Orchestra gave the world premiere of Michael Kamen's orchestral poem *The New Moon in the Old Moon's Arms*, a piece so bad that it can stand as an exemplar for the problems the music world faced in the year 2000. . . . So it was a foolish idea to commission Kamen, given that there was no reason to think he could have produced anything worthwhile. But it went beyond foolishness: It was wrong. The money for commissioning new music is scarce, and Kamen, a well-remunerated Hollywood hack, doesn't need to be dipping

into the paltry amount that's available to composers of serious music. Commissioning him to write something for the NSO amounted to squandering cultural dollars.

And on it went. Leaving aside his distaste for the piece, which is certainly a critic's prerogative, Kennicott simply got so much wrong that I felt compelled to write to the *Post*'s ombudsman. Here are a few excerpts from my commentary:

Mr. Kennicott refers to the work as "a piece so bad it can stand as an exemplar for the problems the music world faced in the year 2000." By whose standard was it so bad? To judge from the letters to the *Post* that were copied to the National Symphony, and the ones printed in the Letters to the Editor on Jan. 22, 2000, audience reaction does not bear out Mr. Kennicott's claim. The only Letter to the Editor printed which seemed negative to the work was signed by someone who admitted to not even being in the hall to hear [Michael] Kamen's piece.

The article goes on to state that "[c]ommissioning him [Kamen] to write something for the NSO amounted to squandering cultural dollars." Clearly Mr. Kennicott has no idea of how the commissioning process works. There is no fixed dollar amount for new music. The orchestra decides what it would like to do regarding premieres and then goes to the appropriate source to solicit the funding. There can be seasons in which there are no premieres or, as happened five years ago, twenty-six. Mr. Kamen was asked to write something that he deemed appropriate for the new millennium. As it happened, there was yet another premiere on the same program, which cost a great deal more than the Kamen.

Also, on Dec. 31, Mr. Kennicott calls the Kamen work "politically trendy" in its use of Native American Indian folklore. In his Jan. 14, 2000, review he states the following: "He [Kamen] steals historical ideas that have no relation to him, his music or his purpose. . . ." In fact, Kamen researched his subject well. He devoted a great deal of time traveling to remote parts of the country. If one applied the same criteria to operatic composers, most would come up short. In the same review, he calls Mr. Kamen's music "offensive aural caricature." Yet, on Dec. 31, he calls the piece "inoffensive to a fault."

"He placed the NSO in an embarrassing position." How? No one in either the administration or orchestra has expressed any thoughts of the kind.

"He further weakened the position of composers who write music with challenging sounds." Once again, how? Is there really a composer out there who altered his/her style of writing because of this piece?

It does seem strange that of all the musical events that took place in this area in the year 2000, Mr. Kennicott chose to focus on this one piece to set a trivial and antagonistic agenda.

I have devoted a lot of space to this incident because it should serve as a warning to us all. Free speech is one thing, but getting correct information to the public is another. Most of the time arts journalists do not expect to be chastised, if only because those on the receiving end are afraid to say something. But once in a while we must stand up to those who get the facts wrong.

If there was one event that could be considered the nadir of my conducting career, it was a March 2010 engagement with the Metropolitan Opera and the furor that accompanied it. In my first book, *Conducting Business*, I wrote extensively about this experience, during which I had published a daily blog about the process of putting together a standard opera with a major opera company. While there is no need to reprint the original blog, I would like to look at how critical response does not necessarily represent the whole story.

There were slightly less than two weeks of preparation, and I was the only one of the principals who had never done *La Traviata* before. Everything was going well until the dress rehearsal, when I found myself thrown by the star's musical antics. By the time we opened, it had turned ugly, and my own contribution was far from satisfactory.

But let's see what the press had to say. As Anthony Tommasini of the *New York Times* stated on March 31, 2010:

> Who would have guessed that a routine revival of *La Traviata* at the Metropolitan Opera could cause such a ruckus? . . . I have seldom heard such faulty coordination between a

conductor and a cast at the Met. . . . On Monday most of [the soprano Angela Gheorghiu's] interpretive touches seemed within the bounds of taste. Still, now and then she was all over the place rhythmically, for example, at the wrenching moment during the ensemble scene with chorus when the courtesan, Violetta, having rejected her lover, Alfredo, is insulted by the hotheaded young man before all the guests at a Paris soiree.

New York Post critic James Jorden referred to the "tentative, clumsy conducting of Leonard Slatkin."

A couple of writers were more sympathetic to me. Tim Smith of the *Baltimore Sun* wrote on June 8, 2010:

The conclusion that a lot of folks made was that Slatkin was not fully prepared and thus caused the many problems heard on that opening night. I only heard (via satellite radio) the last act of that performance, which did not reveal anything horribly amiss. I didn't think the conducting was all that special, however; I like more breathing room in the Act 3 Prelude, for example, than Slatkin allowed.

And Tom Service of London's *Guardian* had this to offer in the June 9, 2010 edition:

It's obvious in hindsight that Slatkin should have trusted his first instincts and refused to conduct *La Traviata*. But when you read in forensic detail on his blog his experiences of the arcane rehearsal process at the Met, the business of having to rehearse without divas and divos, his problems in coordinating the action in the pit with what's going on up there on the stage, you can only feel a wee bit sorry for him. He comes across like a foreigner in a strange, surreal world.

But perhaps this one paragraph in Mr. Tommasini's original *New York Times* review from March 30, 2010 has the most relevance for our purposes here:

> The problem was that the conductor Leonard Slatkin, appearing at the Met for the first time in twelve years, showed up for rehearsals not fully knowing the score. You did not have to believe the reports that spread on opera chat lines to know this. Mr. Slatkin conceded as much on his personal Web site, leonardslatkin.com.

Opera chat lines? Tommasini had admittedly relied on anonymous bloggers for some of his information, not the best idea. Both he and the blogger got the facts wrong. I knew the score intimately and could have conducted it from memory. And nowhere on my blog did I say or mean to imply that I did not know the score. I tried to communicate that I had not conducted the work previously and was looking forward, having studied it carefully, to input from others regarding my ideas.

The role of the chat lines did not stop there.

At about noon on March 31, 2010, my agent called to tell me that the Met wanted me to walk away from the production. And at 10:27 a.m. on April 1, 2010, well before a press release was issued by the Met, the following appeared on the parterre.com blog:

> *La Cieca* has just heard that Leonard Slatkin has been removed from further performances of *Traviata* at the Met.

Obviously, the blogger had access to insider information, perhaps fed to him or her by the same person who served as the anonymous critic during our rehearsals.

There is often more to the story than meets the eye, and I found the experience hurtful.

But it was just a blip on the radar. Two days after the fiasco, I led a concert with the orchestra of the Juilliard School that was met with some of the finest reviews I had ever received. And a few months later Tommasini wrote in the *New York Times* on July 25, 2010 of a subsequent opera performance:

> Unabashedly atonal and teeming with multilayered instrumental writing, *Life Is a Dream* is also a workout for the orchestra. The conductor Leonard Slatkin drew an assured and vibrant performance from the excellent Santa Fe players. That Mr. Slatkin had a wipeout at the Metropolitan Opera last season in Verdi's *Traviata* stemmed from his seeming lack of affinity for the Verdi style. In the right repertory he remains a major musician, as he proved in this impressive outing.

My Detroit period was highly regarded by the critics for the most part. When I arrived, there were two excellent music journalists, but after a couple of years one of the papers dropped the position. Also, during my ninth season, the *Free Press* offered buyouts to its editorial staff, including the excellent music critic, Mark Stryker. This has been the case in almost every American city, and we are all the worse for it. The dissemination of thoughtful artistic discourse is crucial to the survival of our culture. Critics have as much a place in musical society as do performers.

Sometimes the paper's management can be the cause of unpleasantness. In Cleveland the chief critic was taken off covering the orchestra because he wrote negatively about the music director. In Boston, many years ago, one journalist was barred from attending a particular guest conductor's performances because of scathing reviews he had written previously. There have even been instances of the critic's leaving prior to the second half of a concert, or completely skipping the event altogether. But, as with some of the examples above, those are the exception, not the rule. We may not always agree with what the critics write about us, but most of the time they really do get it right.

Let me end with my thoughts on how the relationship between journalists and performers might be strengthened:

1. When there is a new piece on an orchestral program, I recommend critics come to both the dress rehearsal and at least one performance. This would give them a chance to absorb the music, often provide an opportunity to speak to the creator of the work, and allow them to bring a more

thorough understanding of the composer's intention to the public.

2. Critics need to be both objective and subjective in my view. They must characterize performances from dual perspectives: one that expresses the event from the point of view of the audience and one that conveys personal feelings. Sometimes they are one and the same.

3. Every season, it's a good idea for critics to speak to the music director regarding what he or she believes the orchestra has accomplished, and what his or her hopes are in moving forward. This gives the whole season a context within which each program can be written about.

4. These days more and more control is handed over to the artistic administrator. Often program choices do not reflect the tastes of the music director. It is therefore important for music journalists to communicate with management to more fully understand what is taking place.

5. Music journalists should not rely on anonymous sources. If someone wants to leave his or her name off a statement, I don't think it deserves to be published.

6. I prefer the writers to stay until the orchestra leaves the stage. There just might be a surprise encore to write about.

7. Almost every community has a vital arts scene. Coverage and reviews of local artists, not just visiting big names, must be part of a newspaper's agenda.

8. Critics should not be afraid to come backstage after a performance to ask questions if there are areas of the performance that did not compute.

With individual voices, perceptive analyses, and full reportage, the critics remain a vital part of the musical workplace. Very few of us would be where we are today without support from those who write about us. And when those words are harsh or errant, yes, they can hurt. But part of being a musician is the ability to bounce back.

INTERLUDE TWO

——————

LAGNIAPPE

You do not exist to serve the illusion. The illusion exists to serve you.

—Lauren Zimmerman

In the middle of a rehearsal with the Chicago Symphony, we were going over a passage in the first movement of the Rachmaninoff Second Symphony. I made a request of the first violins: "Do you think we could have a portamento here? Not like Kreisler, but more like Heifetz?"

The concertmaster, Sam Magad, replied, "If I could make a portamento like Heifetz, do you think I would be sitting here?"

℞

The conductor Jorge Mester tells this one about himself. He was rehearsing a tricky passage in the scherzo of Schumann's

Second Symphony. The desired result was not forthcoming, so he said to the Philadelphia Orchestra, "This is strange. I have never had trouble with this spot before," to which one of the second violinists responded, "Neither have we."

Klaus Tennstedt was rehearsing the first movement of a Mahler symphony with the London Philharmonic. He innocently asked, "Can we start at bar 5?"

A wag in the viola section said, "Maestro, we don't have measure numbers."

Walter Susskind was presenting one of the early performances of Deryck Cooke's completion of Mahler's Tenth Symphony. At the point near the end of the fourth movement when the muffled drum plays a figure said to represent the cortege at a fireman's funeral, Susskind was not happy with the effect.

"It must sound like a couch—falling."

None of us understood what he meant, but at the next playing of the passage, it sounded absolutely right.

During a concert with the San Francisco Symphony, I was presenting the first local performances of Vaughan Williams's Sixth

Symphony. Since the work was new for the majority of listeners, I decided to say a few words about the piece before playing it.

About three minutes into the talk, a member of the audience stood up and shouted, "Just shut up and play it!"

I told him that I would be speaking for another two minutes, and if he wished to wait outside that would be fine with all of us.

I took the Minnesota Orchestra on a trip to Miami for a new music festival. On one program, we played the Fifth Symphony by Shostakovich. After the performance, a gentleman came backstage and proceeded to give me a rather harsh berating.

"Your orchestra plays too loudly. You must work on your pianissimos."

I forgot about this until a few years later. Emanuel Ax was the soloist in St. Louis in a program that also featured the Third Symphony by Vaughan Williams. This piece is mostly quiet and ends with just the violins holding a very soft A-natural while an offstage soprano delivers a haunting melisma.

There was a knock on my dressing room door, and lo and behold, it was the same gentleman from Miami. I did not recognize him at first, but once he started telling me that the SLSO played too loudly, I remembered him right away.

After a few moments I said, "Sir, we have just completed one of the quietest pieces ever written. We worked very hard on our soft dynamics, and you have no business telling me how this should go."

I pretty much pushed him out the door. Manny was in my room at the time and said, "If I had been in your shoes, I probably would have talked with him for the next two hours."

Jerzy Semkow presented a program that began with the Five Pieces for Orchestra by Webern. I was standing at the back of the hall, and during the very quiet third movement, two elderly ladies got up and headed toward the exit. One of them could clearly be heard saying, "If he didn't want us to hear it, why did he write it?"

In St. Louis, Susskind did a program that consisted of two Eighth Symphonies, those of Mozart and Bruckner. As the audience viewed the quite small forces on stage for the first piece, one member exclaimed, "I don't understand this. They were all here last week!"

The tenor John McCollum told me about an experience he had at New York's Town Hall. He was attending a concert when a man came up to him.

"Are you the singer who performed here last Sunday?" he asked.

"Yes, I am," answered McCollum.

"I thought so," was the comment, and the gentleman walked away.

My mother possessed a wicked tongue. Many musicians would come and play for her, knowing that inevitably she would say something highly critical of the performance.

Jeffrey Siegel was preparing for a recital and decided to go through the full program for her. After an opening Bach suite and a Beethoven sonata, as well as music by Dutilleux and Chopin, Jeffrey waited nervously for Eleanor's comment.

"When did you say you have to play this?" was her only remark.

Some musicians tried to counter my mother's sarcasm by apologizing before she could get a word in. Elmar Oliveira played a recital, and when it was over, everyone headed to the green room to greet him. My mom arrived, the sea of admirers parted, and Elmar decided to take the self-deprecating route.

"Mrs. Slatkin, I know that my thirds were not in tune in the Kreutzer. My upbow staccato just wasn't clean in the Paganini Caprice, and certainly my intonation in the Bach could have been more accurate."

"For Christ's sake, Elmar," my mom said in front of everyone, "You didn't kill anyone!"

For years my mother had wanted to meet Nicolas Slonimsky, the composer and author. There was a rumor that he might have known Modest Altschuler, my mom's uncle, who was an outstanding conductor. Eventually Slonimsky and my mother crossed paths and apparently had a nice conversation.

Slonimsky wondered if she was related to Leonard Slatkin.

When she said yes, the reply was, "Well, at least you have one decent conductor in the family."

My father also had an unusual sense of humor. When he was serving as concertmaster of the orchestra at Warner Bros., where my mother was first cellist, an elaborate practical joke was played on her.

It seems that one portion of the sound track being performed called for a musical saw. It was indeed the workman's tool, played with a bow. Compression and expansion of the blade produce different pitches.

The personnel manager of the orchestra announced to the musicians that they were honored to have the finest living exponent of the saw, who would be playing this all-important cue in the film. He made an entrance, was introduced, and proceeded to take his instrument out of a case that had been especially constructed for the occasion.

The whole orchestra was in on what was about to happen. Only my mom was in the dark.

The soloist sat on a piano bench, planted the saw into the wooden platform on which he was seated, and began to rosin the bow. My mother started to giggle. Everyone else was silent.

At that point, the "sawloist" turned around to the first oboe and asked for an A so he could tune. The moment the sound came out from the virtuoso, my mother began to laugh. My father got up from his chair and went to her saying, "Eleanor, this man is a true artist. Please be respectful."

When she settled down, the conductor signaled for the start of the piece. After a brief introduction by the orchestra, the soloist came in with a toolbox rendition of Camille Saint-Saëns's *The Swan*, a staple of the cello repertoire.

This time my mother burst out in hysterics, tears of laughter streaming down her cheeks. The personnel manager was summoned by the soloist, who said a few words to him; the manager then went to the first cellist.

"Eleanor, you have been asked to leave."

Still in stitches, she picked up her cello and departed. As soon as she reached the soundstage door, the orchestra broke out in sustained laughter, and my mom knew she had been had.

My father had set all this up. They did not speak to each other for about a week after.

Going backstage to say something, especially to a musician friend, when the performance has not been so good requires a great deal of tact. Here are a few lines to use the next time you are in such a situation:

> "I never heard anything like it."
> "Ahh, the slow movement!"
> "Your instrument sounds wonderful."
> "Very interesting choice of tempi."
> "I never understood this piece until now."
> "Can't wait to hear it in a better acoustic."

Arthur Fiedler came off the stage after a concert in St. Louis. I was waiting for him, scotch in hand. He took it, downed the whole glass in one swig, and said, "That's one concert closer to the grave."

In Washington the former music director Mstislav Rostropovich returned to play a benefit concert. His repertoire included the First Cello Concerto by Shostakovich. The piece begins with a four-note motif played by the soloist alone. This sets the tempo for the whole movement.

I was conducting, and Slava said that he would take the tempo from me. I picked up the score and, pointing to the composer's dedication to Rostroprovich himself, countered, "*I* will take the tempo from *you*."

Favorite conductor joke:

A man goes into the butcher shop and explains that he is having a dinner party that night and wants something special to serve up. The butcher says that he has an outstanding selection of brains.

"I can let you have these for $1 a pound. They are the brains of a tenor."

The man says that this is an important gathering of people, requiring something of higher quality.

The butcher then offers the brains of a pianist for $3 a pound.

Again, the customer says that there must be a better cut.

Going to the next level, the butcher points to a pan with more brains.

"These are of concertmasters. I can sell you this for $5 a pound."

The man says, "Just tell me which brains are the most exclusive."

The butcher asks, "How many people are going to attend?"

"Eight altogether."

After thinking for a moment, the proprietor says, "I have enough to be able to offer the brains of a conductor."

"How much?"

"$200 a pound," the butcher replies.

"I don't understand. The tenor was $1, the pianist $3, and the concertmaster $5. Why are the conductor's brains so expensive?"

"Do you know how many conductors it takes to get a pound of brains?"

In my second term as President, Leonard Slatkin, conductor of the Washington National Symphony, asked me if I would direct the orchestra in Sousa's "Stars and Stripes Forever" at the Kennedy Center. He told me all I had to do was wave the baton more or less in time and the musicians would do the rest. He even offered to bring me a baton and show me how to hold it. When I told him that I'd be delighted to do it but that I wanted him to send me the score of the march so I could review it, he almost dropped the phone. But he brought the score and the baton. When I stood before the orchestra I was nervous, but we got into it, and away we went. I hope Mr. Sousa would have been pleased.

—President Bill Clinton, *My Life*

What he did not write was that after the performance, President Clinton said to me, "That's the first time I ever got one hundred people to do what I wanted."

My debut with the Boston Symphony produced this unexpected gem. Tchaikovsky's Second Symphony was the main work on the program. I was having trouble getting the first violins together in a passage during the finale. After three tries at it, the concertmaster extraordinaire Joseph Silverstein stood up, turned around, and said, "And what do we have on the fifth stand, a couple of Ayatollahs?"

Needless to say, I was stunned, but Joey had the total respect of all the musicians and could speak his mind at any time.

John Browning told the story of a continuing feud between the conductor Erich Leinsdorf and New York Philharmonic's principal oboist, Harold Gomberg.

The culmination took place during a rehearsal of John's signature piece, the Barber Piano Concerto. There is a beautiful and lengthy solo for the oboe in the first movement. After much bickering between Leinsdorf and Gomberg, the conductor asserted:

> Mr. Gomberg, I have an idea. Why don't you put the oboe down, then come here and conduct? I will step off the podium and take your place. This already assures us one thing: the oboe playing will improve!

Most orchestras are blessed with incredible stage crews. They make our job much less stressful and usually are fully engaged with the artists. In St. Louis, Leroy Stone served as the head of the group for quite a long time. He had seen it all.

Alexander Gibson was in town, and among the pieces he was conducting was the Beethoven Fifth. Sir Alex tried to jest with Leroy.

"Mr. Stone, do you think I should do this piece from memory?"

"Sir Alex, *I* could do this piece from memory!"

Succeeding Leroy was Marty McManus. In this case, the encounter in question was with the great violinist Henryk Szeryng. The somewhat temperamental Pole was hemming and hawing backstage prior to his performance. Marty tried to be diplomatic.

"Maestro, it's time to start."

"I am the Ambassador to Mexico. Please address me as such."

"I'll call you anything you want," Marty responded, "just get your ass onstage!"

Szeryng also had an odd sense of humor. We were rehearsing the Mendelssohn Concerto when, in the middle of the first movement, he stopped the orchestra and said:

"Ladies and gentlemen, Maestro Slatkin is not a good conductor."

I groaned, as did the orchestra. Waiting for the other shoe, this is what we got:

"He is a great conductor!"

We all groaned again.

During a trip to Japan, when I was working with the NHK Symphony Orchestra, there was a jarring tremor during a dress rehearsal. One of the overhead stage lights fell down and landed near the soloist, the violist Yuri Bashmet. This caused one musician to remark simply, "Earthquake. Big one!" Then another chimed in, saying in perfect English, "That's the first time the earth has ever moved for a violist."

Once in a while I can get off a zinger or two. Here are a few examples of which I am particularly proud.

"Violins—why are you using so little bow? You paid for the whole thing."

"While it is still legal, would you mind playing with vibrato?"

At a performance at the Festival Hall in London, a cell phone went off between the first two movements of a Chopin concerto. I turned to the audience and said, "Please answer it and tell them that I will be available in about twenty minutes."

I had a couple of rough moments with the Los Angeles Philharmonic when my career was just beginning. They tried to take advantage of having known me since I was little. Once, a violinist wondered if I was going to use all the rehearsal time. I asked him why he needed to know.

"Some of us have film sessions out at Warner's and we want to make sure we get there on time."

This is one of the last things any conductor wants to hear, so my rejoinder was, "You know, this program is not so easy. We might even need to go into overtime."

On another occasion, we were rehearsing the Bartók First Piano Concerto with Peter Serkin. There had been a coordination problem in one passage, and the first bassoon rather brusquely asked me to conduct a particular bar in one beat, just as Zubin Mehta had done a couple seasons ago.

All I could say was, "I am sure it went very well then, but I do the bar in two. And by the way, what difference does it make to you? You don't come in until seven measures later!"

Finally, of all the compliments and criticisms I have ever been given, none is more memorable, and uncomfortable, than something André Previn said to me after a rehearsal of his Guitar Concerto. Even though we had known each other for many years, he had never seen me conduct.

"Leonard, your beat is so clear even Helen Keller could follow it!"

PART FOUR

———

WRAPPING UP

Sometimes ends are in fact beginnings; beginnings ends.

—Anna Godbersen, *Splendor*

SLATKIN ON SLATKIN

Art attracts us only by what it reveals of our most secret self.

—Jean-Luc Godard

In my first book, *Conducting Business*, I wrote a concluding chapter answering ten of the most frequently asked questions I receive. This time, I am going to interview myself and try to ask questions that are, at least so far, very rarely put to me. Not all of them are about music.

1. When you turned seventy, did you begin to think about your legacy?

There are some elements of my musical life that I am particularly proud of. Founding the youth orchestra in St. Louis, starting the conducting institute in Washington, and helping to forge a path in the post-strike era of the Detroit Symphony come to mind. My advocacy for the music of the United States has also been a source of joy.

Perhaps because of these and other choices I have made, there are some who don't take me so seriously as a true master of the standard repertoire. Granted, there are areas of weakness in virtually every musician's life, but for the most part, I feel that my approach to the performance of standard works has matured over the years, and that my viewpoint has become more focused and personal.

2. Which orchestra do you feel will be most identified with you?

Even with lengthy histories, orchestras are usually associated with just one music director, sometimes two. No matter how successful other directors have been, there are some names that are simply synonymous with the ensembles they led.

New York will always be Bernstein's orchestra. Philadelphia is a shared one between Stokowski and Ormandy. Cleveland, hands down, remains the orchestra of George Szell. Berlin is still the hallowed ground of Herbert von Karajan. Reiner and Solti were the Chicago duo. There are only a few living conductors who have already achieved this degree of identity with their orchestras. Michael Tilson Thomas in San Francisco is one of them.

And perhaps I am another as music director in St. Louis.

Why would these examples be the case? We all had lengthy tenures with our respective ensembles. We all transformed the way our orchestras were seen, both locally and worldwide. Each of us had a vision for how we wished our musicians to be recognized, and we stuck with it. Even though I did some things in other cities that were truly memorable accomplishments for me, it was in St. Louis that I experienced the most growth and helped to initiate the most change. Perhaps I will be considered pivotal in Detroit, but at least as of this writing, the DSO is still Neeme Järvi's—or even Paul Paray's—to many.

3. You never embraced some styles and certain schools of musical thought. Why not?

It is important to understand that not every musician can play every style with equal success. You might try them out early on, and even develop a strong feeling for something you did not care about earlier, but there are always categories of music that simply remain foreign to you.

For example, composers of the Second Viennese School and their disciples do not interest me too much. Like many listeners, I find it difficult to connect emotionally with the highly chromatic music of those who employ strict twelve-tone contrapuntal techniques. Also, too many pieces in this style sound pretty much the same. Rigorous counterpoint can of course also be found in the music of Bach, Brahms, Hindemith, and Piston, to name just a few, but these composers found ways to express highly individualized voices.

Music of the Baroque era used to be part of my repertoire. Then, as the number of scholars and musicians dealing with "historically informed" performance practice grew, I found myself at a dead end. There were too many conflicting ideas about how to play this music. I appreciate the effort to replicate how things might have sounded a few hundred years ago, but one cannot listen with the ears of those earlier centuries. If you have heard Stravinsky or Bartók, it changes how you hear Handel or Telemann.

And, as Sir Neville Marriner liked to say, "If Bach had a modern toilet, he would have used it."

4. There was a period when your personal life came under public scrutiny. Did this affect your music-making?

There is no question that I have had my share of unhappy times. Three marriages fell apart, two of them quite quickly. And the third was spent grappling with the choice between career and family life. A much-publicized affair hit the press and may have even been responsible for some lost opportunities in the musical world.

Being on the road is particularly tempting when it comes to dangerous liaisons. You are away from home, and there are people with whom you come into contact who need similar companionship. Somehow you believe that you can get away with stepping out of bounds, and that all those other people who get caught were just foolish. All of a sudden you become the fool.

And yes, it does make a difference to your art. Your focus changes, and you do not concentrate in quite the same way. There is always a voice in your head, sometimes making you feel guilty and other times plotting the next connection you will make. No amount of therapy, counseling, or discussion can keep you from what almost seems like an addiction. But the show goes on, even when you are served divorce papers five minutes prior to the start of the concert. (That happened.)

I am terribly envious of my music colleagues who have managed to walk a straight path. Maybe they just found the right person at an early age. And possibly they were more committed to the family ethic thanks to their own upbringing. My family was dysfunctional, and this must have rubbed off on me.

Walter Susskind said to me, "Listen to what I have to say, not the way I act." That could easily be my motto as well.

5. Tell us about your personal life now.

As I moved toward my late sixties, my personal life changed for the better. My wife, Cindy McTee, understands me and my various quirks. It took four tries, but in the end, I found the perfect partner in Cindy. Some people get it right the first time, and then there are the rest of us.

My son, Daniel, has been a constant pleasure, even though the itinerant life of a conductor made it difficult for me to be there for him all the time. He is his own man and possibly, like his father, not having a paternal figure around all the time contributed to his remarkable independence. I did try to guide him as best I could. He seems to be doing very well.

6. Do you ever speak with other conductors?

It is not that we dislike each other, but usually time and place come into play: very rarely am I in the same city at the same time as other maestri. Yes, if it is New York, London, or Berlin, there may be the opportunity, but only if there is time.

Occasionally I get to do a festival where there might be several conductors. When circumstances permit, we go to each other's concerts and sometimes grab a bite after the performance. Most of the discussion these days is about the state of the musical world, but every so often we might talk about a few details within the canon.

What is best about these brief encounters is the stories that we tell each other, usually about our upbringings and musical influences. We do not speak too much about today's conductors. But we do worry that some of the kids on the podium are simply moving too fast and will burn out.

7. You haven't ventured into the opera pit very often. Why not?

A few years ago, when Riccardo Muti fell from the podium and I jumped in as a substitute, I went to visit him in the hospital. We had only met once, years ago, so it was time spent getting to know each other. At one point he said, "You aren't a man of the theater, are you?"

I explained about my background being rooted in chamber music and orchestral repertoire. He took it in stride, but I wondered if he considered this a deficiency in my career.

I have done many productions in small as well as great houses. I have conducted at The Met three times, Chicago Lyric four times, Paris Opera once, Stuttgart once, Santa Fe twice, St. Louis twice, and Hamburg once, as well as several other theaters. In addition, I have always been an active promoter of opera in concert.

But I admit to not having embraced all of opera. Works that require the conductor to be more or less an accompanist for the entire evening do not interest me. And I won't even go into the productions themselves.

There has long been a misguided theory that the majority of great maestri began their musical journeys in the pit. That may have been true at one time, but it changed dramatically in the twentieth century. You can go back to Stokowski, Koussevitzky, and Ormandy, to name only a few, who did not get their starts in opera houses. Today some conductors choose to do both opera and concert work, while others focus primarily on one or the other. I came to the stage works relatively late, and I quickly determined that I would not focus on this area of the musical world.

Still, the experience I did have was always worthwhile, and dealing with all the moving parts was exciting. But my preference will always be to stand in front of a symphony orchestra, making up our own stories as a piece of abstract music goes forward.

The only regret I have as a conductor is that I will never lead a work as great as any of the late Beethoven quartets, the Schubert String Quintet with two cellos, or the Brahms C Minor Piano Quartet.

8. There has been a lot of discussion about discrimination in the orchestral workplace. Do you find this to be the case?

There is certainly a long way to go, but women, those in the LGBT community, and other minority groups have become more accepted in the field. The one exception, at least in terms of conductors, seems to be African Americans.

There have always been gay musicians, whether composers, performers, or conductors. "The love that dare not speak its name" certainly accounted for more than a few artists' being excluded from elite positions, including Leonard Bernstein with respect to the Boston Symphony. But as we moved into the 1960s, acceptance became more generous, and today the issue of a musician's sexual orientation rarely surfaces.

When I gave the Boston premiere of John Corigliano's Symphony No. 1 in 1993, there was an objection from two of the musicians in the BSO. The work was inspired by the AIDS quilt, and there were some in the orchestra who refused to perform because of the subject matter. But that was almost a quarter of a century ago.

Women on the podium are still a relatively new phenomenon, even though pioneers such as Antonia Brico, Nadia Boulanger, and Sarah Caldwell paved the way for the new crop of female conductors. At the forefront of today's maestri, Marin Alsop has been the standard-bearer, but there are many others as well, including Susanna Mälkki, Mirga Gražinytė-Tyla, and Barbara Hannigan.

Can we expect parity with their male counterparts in terms of music directorships? That really depends on how many are studying, something that will take several more years to evolve. The same applies to composers.

I believe that one of the difficulties faced by women conductors has something to do with attempts to emulate their male counterparts as opposed to just being themselves. All of us started out trying to imitate those (mostly men) we saw and heard, and so it was for female conductors. But today's generation of women on the podium are beginning to exhibit true individuality. The glass ceiling may not have been broken in terms of music directors of major orchestras, but that will soon change.

For black conductors, it is more difficult. Years of repression kept so many out of the classical music field, once considered the bastion of white men. There are relatively few African American applicants to music schools and even fewer role models. Dean Dixon and Henry Lewis helped break barriers, but they have been forgotten by most. Still, I see encouraging signs, owing primarily to outreach programs many orchestras have instituted. All it takes is one person to succeed and others will follow.

Roger O. Doyle made an amusing comment about discrimination of a different type: "I have always insisted that left-handed persons learn to beat the patterns with their right hand—which, I believe, made them even better conductors because they also had the advantage of very expressive left-hand gestures for adding the details of music-making."

9. **Now that you are stepping down from your music directorships, there are those who believe you are retiring. Is that true?**

Certainly not! What I am doing is bringing an end to the administrative part of my conducting career. There was a time when I thought that this was one of my great strengths. Problem solving, putting seasons together, and hiring musicians was an exhilarating part of the job.

The world has changed, but in many ways I have not. In the United States music directors now have less authority than they used to. Although I think that the players' role within an orchestral institution should be increased, ultimately artistic matters need to be decided by the music director. Most of us try to accommodate the concerns of marketing and publicity departments and acknowledge fiscal constraints, but being so active in this area holds little interest for me now.

In Europe, with the two directorships I held, I never really felt as though I was in complete control of the ship. Guest artists, conductors, and programs were usually selected with my approval rather than through my initiative. In these posts I didn't feel like the true leader. But I did not mind relinquishing some of the responsibilities that related to being a music director. Auditions, board meetings, and fund-raising were beginning to take a toll, both emotionally and physically.

I expect to continue relationships with almost all the orchestras I have worked with in the past, especially as I look forward to celebrating my seventy-fifth birthday in 2019. I compose more now, and I am also trying my hand at arranging and transcribing.

If I conduct about thirty weeks a year, that is plenty for me. And it gives me time to enjoy parts of the world I have never seen.

10. You once said that you despised competitions in music, and yet you are now involved in several. What changed your mind?

My original opinion has not changed, just my view of the reality of the situation. It started when I realized that listening to auditions to fill vacancies in an orchestra was just another form of competition adjudication. There was no getting around it.

In 2013 I was asked to conduct the final two rounds for the Van Cliburn International Piano Competition in Fort Worth, Texas. Not having to pass judgment seemed an interesting way to get an idea of how a major competition was run. There were the usual controversies about jury members also being teachers, pianists who could wow audiences but might burn out right away, and whether the audience should be given a public forum for voicing their preferences.

At the end of the finals I was asked to give my opinion to the jury. I spoke about the rehearsal process with each of the finalists and gave my take on who should be first, second, and third. As it turned out, in each case the jury agreed with me. It was, overall, a very good experience, and a year later I was asked if I would take on the role of jury chairman.

I agreed, but only on the condition that I could still conduct the finals. Perhaps my thinking was that I could help make a difference in identifying those who might actually make decent careers for themselves.

Being a participant as well as a judge made all the difference in the world for me. I still believe that there are too many competitions and that they rarely produce lasting results. But I also realize that for many young musicians, this is an important avenue to success.

11. Lastly, how can we effectively encourage young people to take an interest in the fine arts?

Of course, that should have been the first question. Again, I am taking a point of view reflecting the American landscape. There was a time when most children were provided with instruction in the arts. When I arrived in Detroit, the acting supervisor of schools proudly remarked that 30 percent of all young people in the public schools had music education. I immediately shot back that this meant 70 percent did not.

Another problem is that we have become visually oriented to the point where most music seems to need an image to accompany the sound. That's unfortunate, because it discourages listeners from imagining their own pictures.

Many orchestras have not helped the situation by introducing a video component into the concert proceedings. Often, as evidenced by NASA footage that is used to supplement Gustav Holst's suite *The Planets*, the visuals simply do not jibe with what the composer intended. I had the unfortunate experience of performing Beethoven's Ninth at the Hollywood Bowl accompanied by an abstract video presentation featuring vines growing over a parking meter.

Certainly there is room for artistic liberty, but it must be balanced against the composer's intention. My rule of thumb here is that we must present our product as if no one in the audience has experienced it before. Keeping traditions alive is therefore crucial to having an educated public.

It all starts with the family sharing all kinds of listening experiences. We are at least two generations away from a time when early arts education came from the home or houses of worship. Parents need to hear what their kids have on their iPods, and kids need to listen to what their parents heard as young people. But I recommend just listening, not watching! And never, ever criticize.

It would be helpful if more parents would go to their school boards and actively promote all kinds of music education initiatives.

One idea is to fold arts education into the history curriculum. All things have a context, so talking about what was going on during the time Beethoven wrote the "Eroica," or when Monet painted his water lilies, can bring additional meaning and excitement into the classroom.

TWO CODETTAS
AND A LAST
WORD

*The principle of the endless melody is the perpetual be-
coming of a music that never had any reason for starting,
any more than it has any reason for ending.*

—Igor Stravinsky

I t has not been my habit to cancel engagements. I've done so
only a couple of times, and the reasons had to do with health
and safety. The first is obvious, the second less so.

In mid-2001 I was scheduled to conduct the Israel Philharmonic, an orchestra I had led four times previously. This was a
time of greater than usual tension in the Middle East. The typical
inflammatory rhetoric was ratcheted up a couple of notches, and
artists scheduled to perform in that region were considering
other options.

At the time I was the music director in Washington, which
gave me more access to information than some of my colleagues
had. About three months before my trip I was at a dinner party
attended by former Secretary of State Colin Powell. Since we

had struck up an acquaintance over the previous few years, it seemed appropriate to ask him what I should do. His response was for me to wait a little longer, and he would advise as the situation developed.

Six weeks later I was at another dinner, this one with Powell's wife, Alma. She came over to my table and whispered in my ear, "Colin says you are not to go to Israel." That was all she said, and ultimately I agreed. The next day I instructed my agent to cancel the trip.

I had other reasons for canceling. At the time my son was only five years old. My wife and I discussed the pros and cons of my going and decided that the stress of an almost-three-week trip to the region would be too much for everyone. It would have been different if we did not have a child.

The response came from the IPO's executive director, Avi Shoshani. He was furious.

"Tel Aviv is a safer city than New York," he said. "You are no friend of Israel!" He then added, "I am also canceling your appearance at the Verbier Festival."

I knew that several other artists, including Anne-Sophie Mutter, had also chosen not to go to Israel at this time. I could not say anything to others about the advice from the Secretary of State, not that it would have swayed Avi's opinion one bit.

Sure, New York was dangerous. I was mugged twice during my student years at Juilliard. I knew people who were put in the hospital because of violent incidents, and I saw a man shot in Times Square. But at that time, a few months before 9/11, we did not consider New York or other American cities vulnerable to threats from abroad. Israel was a hotbed of terrorist activity, and although the armed forces of that country were among the finest in the world, they could not possibly prevent a determined suicide bomber from wreaking havoc.

Avi served as an administrator at the Verbier Festival. In its early stages the Swiss Music Academy had some of the leading artists and teachers in the musical world. How my decision to cancel the Middle East appearance had anything to do with a musical gathering in Switzerland was incomprehensible, especially in light of the fact that he chose to retain the services of Mutter, who was also looking out for family interests in her decision not to travel to Israel at that time.

A few months after my cancellation, there was a devastating bombing in Tel Aviv. A lone suicide attacker destroyed the Dolphinarium discotheque, a gathering place for young Israelis and Russian émigrés. Twenty-one people were killed, and more than 150 were seriously injured.

Powell had been correct in urging caution. It was clear that not only Israeli locals but also foreigners were going to be targets. And had I chosen to go to Israel, it would have been exactly at the time of that horrific incident.

Some fourteen years later I ran into Avi at a festival in Warsaw. He turned his back when he saw me. He was speaking with a couple of people, so I decided to go up to him. We said hello, but the greeting was frozen in an Arctic chill. The next day, as part of the festival, we both attended a church service that included music of Krzystof Penderecki. Avi did not bother to say anything at all.

Sometimes one accepts a date out of curiosity and perhaps the promise of a big fee. Such was the case in the late 1970s, when I was asked to do a pair of concerts with an orchestra in Mexico City. My career was beginning to take off, and it was possible to be more selective in my choice of where to conduct. Several people had cautioned me about Mexico, explaining that often artists are not paid and leave empty-handed. Thus warned, my manager worked out a deal dictating that I was to be paid in cash prior to the second performance.

South of the border I went. During my youth in Los Angeles, smog was just starting to be a problem, but in Mexico City it was already very serious. And the altitude did not help. Not much was known about the schedule for the week. What I did know was that the program included Handel's *Water Music*, Joaquín Rodrigo's *Fantasía para un gentilhombre* for guitar and orchestra, and Stravinsky's *The Rite of Spring*.

The morning of the first rehearsal I was taken by car not to an auditorium or even a school, but to an abandoned garage. This is where the orchestra practiced. My Spanish was nonexistent, but there were several Americans in the orchestra, a couple of whom I had gone to school with, who did speak the language. We started off with the Stravinsky.

It is almost always my practice to play through a work right away so the orchestra can get used to me and vice versa. But this time I had to stop about five bars in. The score calls for two bass clarinetists, both of whom play at the same time. One was missing.

"Where is the second bass clarinet player?" I asked.

"He is at the dentist."

"Well, we will really need him. Will he be here for the second rehearsal?"

"Yes, he should be finished by then."

The morning was agonizing. I had serious doubts about getting through the piece by the time of the performance. Lunchtime arrived, and I needed to know when the second rehearsal would commence. The personnel manager said, "Maybe two or three hours from now. It depends on how long they want to eat."

Eventually, the musicians returned, and we started again at the opening of the Stravinsky. There was still only one bass clarinet player, but it was not the same musician who had played during the morning rehearsal.

"Where is the second bass clarinetist?" I inquired.

"This man is our second bass clarinet player. You said that is who you wanted."

"But the piece needs two at the same time."

"You didn't say that," he replied archly. "You asked for the second bass clarinet player, and there he is."

Then I asked, "What happened to the musician who was here this morning?"

"He went home. He did not think he was needed."

"Stravinsky wants two," I countered.

We would not have both musicians together until the dress rehearsal. The whole week went like this.

Performances were on Saturday night and Sunday morning. At the dress rehearsal I was surprised to see a battery of television cameras present. No one had bothered to tell me that the concert was to be shown live all over the country. We really were not ready at all, and I had visions of disaster on the scale of the Hindenburg.

The first half went more or less without incident. Nothing great, but no major collisions. Then came *The Rite*.

Somehow, we got through Part One without having to stop. Still, I knew that the Sacrificial Dance was coming, and we had never managed a play-through in rehearsal. But lo and behold, when it began, things looked like we might just make it. That was when the trouble really started.

Just after the first sixteen measures or so, a distant but audible male voice could be heard singing offstage. It got closer and closer until a highly inebriated construction worker ambled onto the stage, clearly intent on making his performance debut with us. Three violinists got up, tackled him, and dragged the poor man off the platform.

At this point I was not about to stop conducting. We were so close to the end. With the last crunch of sound, the audience was stone-cold silent. I dropped my stick onto the music stand in the hopes that they would understand that the piece had ended. Gradually, the applause started, but it was halfhearted at best.

In my dressing room about eight journalists came by to ask me what I thought about the intruder. Now I was in full sarcasm mode and decided to have some fun with the incident.

"You know, years ago I remember reading that this ballet was originally conceived as an opera about pagan Russia. Now that I have actually experienced the cries during the sacrifice, I think I will do some investigating to see if perhaps one could reconstruct what might have been heard back then."

They bought it.

You would think this would be the end of the story. But no way.

When I got back to my hotel, I called American Airlines and asked them about flights to the United States the next afternoon. Originally I had planned to stay in Mexico for a few days of holiday, but now my goal was to get out as soon as possible.

The operator asked me where I wanted to go and I said, "Wherever your first flight is, around 2:30 in the afternoon." In a few minutes I had booked a ticket for Dallas, knowing that I could transfer to St. Louis at some point later in the day. Then I spoke with an American trumpet player in the orchestra and asked him if he knew a reliable taxi driver who could get me to the airport quickly. One was lined up, and my plan was to go from podium to car, literally.

The concert began at 11:00, and I arrived a half hour early. This was the day I was to receive my fee. Standing in front of my dressing room were three men in black suits. We went into the room, and the first one pulled out a brown envelope containing my salary in American dollars. Mind you, this was the largest fee I had ever received for any conducting date. I was asked to count it, and indeed, it was all there.

Then the second gentleman asked me to do it again; a third counting of the cash followed, all well and good. I had my money. But a new dilemma now presented itself. What was I going to do with all that cash while the concert was going on? With all the tales of theft, graft, corruption, and of course frustrated opera singers coming onstage, I certainly could not take the chance of leaving it in the room.

The only solution was to divide it up and stuff it in every available pocket. Looking like a darker version of the Michelin man, I went onstage and did the concert loaded with moolah. Now all I cared about was whether the taxi driver would be there at the end. He was, and my one suitcase had already been loaded into what looked like a relic from the 1940s. The drive to the airport was more like Mr. Toad's Adventure at the old Disneyland, with my driver actually using sidewalks when the traffic was too thick to pass. We made it in plenty of time. I have never been so glad to step into Texas.

There are some who do not believe a word of this story, but in 2012, while I was shopping in a hardware store in suburban Detroit, two people came up to me and introduced themselves. I did not recognize them by either sight or name, but they revealed that they had been in the orchestra in Mexico when all that went on—and they verified almost every point.

I really should not be so hard on Mexico. My wife and I visited recently, and we very much enjoyed the Mexican people, as well as their art, food, museums, and beaches. However, any rites that were performed during our stay did not involve bass clarinets, improvisational singing, or cash-lined pockets.

As I write this, I am about to turn seventy-three years old. This means I have been a professional musician for fifty-six years and a conductor for fifty-two of them. My father died at the age of forty-seven, his father at fifty-six. My mother's side of the family was longer-lived.

Unfortunately, my genetics favor my dad's side of the family. I have had a heart attack, prostate removal, various other replacement parts added, and some taken away. The never-ending battle of the bulge continues, and I have the usual aches and pains that come with growing older.

It is music that has kept me going. It is difficult to predict what the future holds, but as I mentioned in an earlier chapter, I do know that I want to cut back, and therefore I am leaving my decades-old role of music director. The plan is to guest conduct for about twenty-eight to thirty weeks a year.

My website has become a passion for me and a great place to hone my writing skills. Cindy and I share an enthusiasm for all aspects of our lives, and we do almost everything together. It is rare to find us apart. My son, an inspiration to me, has moved into the field of composing for television and movies, thereby bringing me somewhat full circle with my childhood.

It has been a great life so far. Whatever setbacks I encountered were all met with a positive attitude about the future. For the most part, I consider it a life well lived, with lessons learned almost every day. Hopefully this will all continue until I can no longer physically or mentally perform at the level I deem appropriate. When that day comes, I will simply stop.

Now it is time to reap the rewards of whatever it is that I may have accomplished. Just doing what I want and when I wish to do it is paramount. Life, in its myriad expressions, is there to be enjoyed.

But of one thing there is no question in my mind: I have been privileged to participate in one of the best professions in the world.

INDEX

education, arts, 6, 273–75
  1812 Overture (Tchaikovsky),
    Fourth of July concerts
    inclusion of, 205–7
elitism, 178
L'enfant et les sortilèges (Ravel), 53–54
Erb, Donald, 22–23
"Eroica." *See* Symphony No. 3
  (Beethoven)
ethnicity, of orchestra members, 119
Europe
  preconcert rituals in, 99–100
  running orchestras in, 15
European Union Sound Act of 2008,
  Slatkin, Leonard, article on,
  170–73
The Exorcist, Slatkin, Leonard,
  recordings for, 38

Fairouz, Mohammed, 28
Fandangos (Sierra), 25
"Fanfare for an Uncommon Man"
  (Slatkin, L.), 154–59
Fanfares for the Uncommon
  Woman (Tower), 23
Faulkner, William, man's
  endurance quote of, vi
Fiedler, Arthur, 252
  1812 Overture performances of, 206
Fifth Symphony (Prokofiev), award-
  winning recording of, 35
Fifth Symphony (Tchaikovsky),
  audience applause during,
  169–70
films
  putting music together with, 97
  Slatkin, Leonard, article on, 203–5
  Slatkin, Leonard, recordings for,
  38
  Williams, John, work for, 96–98

Final Alice (Del Tredici), 21
financial information, availability
  of, 149
fine arts, encouraging young
  people to take interest in,
  273–75
First Cello Concerto
  (Shostakovich), 252–53
First Piano Concerto (Brahms),
  48–49
First Piano Concerto (Camilo), 25
First Violin Concerto
  (Shostakovich), audience
  applause during, 212
fiscal responsibility, coupling
  creative vision with, 183–93
flowers, at concerts, 108
Forbes, Malcolm, 111
Ford Motor Company Fund, 190,
  208
4'33" (Cage), 31
Fourth of July concerts, Slatkin,
  Leonard, article on, 205–7
France
  running orchestras in, 15
  Slatkin, Leonard, early
  conducting in, 9–10
  Slatkin, Leonard, Orchestre
  National de Lyon conducting
  work in, 11–18
Frank, Anne, beauty quote of, vi
French, Slatkin, Leonard, learning
  of, 9, 18
fund-raising, creative methods of,
  183–93

gay musicians, 269–70
gender, of orchestra members, 119
generations, musical gap between,
  159–62